House on the Lake:

Poems and Stories

Also by Wilma (Hartley) Daugherty:

Fragments: Stories of Another Time
There was a Time
Along the Way
Merrygold

House on the Lake:

Poems and Stories

Wilma (Hartley) Daugherty

Drinian Press/
Huron, Ohio

House on the Lake: Poems and Stories

Drinian Press LLC
P.O. Box 63
Huron, Ohio 44839

www.DrinianPress.com.

Cover design and photo by Drinian Press
Edited by Nancy Brady Smith

Library of Congress Control Number: 2014954547

ISBN-10: 1941929001
ISBN-13: 978-1-941929-00-1

DrinianPress.com
Printed in the United States

House on the Lake:
Poems and Stories

Table of Contents

House on the Lake:

Poems and Stories

There Was A Time

There was a time
When I sat cross-legged on the floor
And read poetry aloud,
While my young husband
painted a portrait
of the lovely Ruby,
Ruby of the pink cheeks
and innocent eyes.
She wore calico, I remember,
and her Robert placed a rose
in her soft brown hair.
Robert-a genius no less-
sang *Funiculi, Finiculae*,
Exuberant, off-key
as he beat the fudge,
Fudge that wouldn't get hard.
We ate it from the pan
with spoons
and laughed and dripped chocolate.

Weird!

I hesitated to write this for fear of being forever considered a weirdo in the minds of my friends. But what happened was so amazing and yes, weird, that I have to tell it just like it happened. Perhaps someone has an explanation.

First of all I seldom drink anything stronger than coffee. I am not on drugs and never have been. I had not been asleep or dreaming or looking at old pictures. I was just doing everyday things, washing dishes, putting away clothes, making the bed. I was neither sad nor particularly happy. It was an ordinary day.

I was beside the dresser in my bedroom on Mansfield Avenue. I turned to go out of the room.

Suddenly I am standing in the bedroom of the log house on Cincinnati Avenue. I smell the cedar logs, feel the tile floor under my feet. I have come in from the other room to get my rings. I am wearing a long red robe reaching down to my bare feet. My hair is longer and smoother. It is Christmas morning.

In the other room Bill is sitting on the floor beside the tree. He is smiling at the children.

Eight year old Marty is wearing a blue and white robe. It has a small collar trimmed with a white ruffle. I smile at her tousled red curls. But who has time to brush curls on a magic Christmas morning!

I am watching three year old Michael. He has such beautiful eyes and black hair like silk. He is wearing his new red plaid bathrobe. He has written to Santa asking for a robe because his Dad had one. Now he has put it on with the collar turned wrong side out and the fringed belt dangling on the floor.

Santa left them a small record player that plays *45's*. They are enchanted with it. They are playing *Lisbon Antigua*, lovely sweet music, holding hands and dancing. Bill finds it very funny.

The logs overhead are wrapped in tinsel. Bill has painted a Christmas scene on the entire picture window. It shows camels and the three wise men following the bright star.

The small tree sparkles with silver lights, bright ornaments, and funny little things the kids made. A lopsided angel keeps watch over us. The large braided rug makes the room look cozy and comfortable.

I am completely filled with happiness. I have everything, I think. I have it all, a husband I adore, two bright healthy kids, our small house.

Now I will go out, sit on the floor, and lean on Bill. I reach down for my rings. My hands are young and slender.

I turn to go and---

I am standing in my room on Mansfield Avenue.

Alone.

Conkle's Hollow

To go back to Conkle's Hollow again and be able to recapture the adventure and excitement we had always found there seemed highly unlikely. Four years before, doctors had told Bill he would probably never walk again due to his MS, an opinion that he simply didn't accept.

Hocking State Forest is one of the most spectacular places in Ohio, with six State Parks within its forest. My husband Bill and I had camped at various times in all of them with our children and grandchildren.

Back at Hocking Forest, we decided to hike in Conkle's Hollow. The trail winds between towering cliffs, leading over small streams, between huge boulders. The gorge is heavily wooded with ancient trees and a tangle of small growth and rare vegetation. A recent tornado had ripped through leaving trees across the trail.

We all decided that Bill would stay in the rest area at the head of the trail. It is a quiet and pleasant place with benches where he could sit and simply enjoy the outdoors. However, Bill didn't consider this plan even for a moment. He was going to hike with us.

He is wearing a red and white plaid shirt that hangs on his six-foot frame like a scarecrow. His brown slacks are cinched around his waist—slacks that fit him thirty pounds ago. His cap says, "Best Dad." His hair, once dark brown, is now white, showing only around his ears and on his neck. His shoes are heavy brown walking shoes, and he carries a stout cane. Only his smile is unchanged.

So, undaunted we start out in a long procession, my grandchildren Andrea and Matthew, each with a friend, my daughter Marty and son Michael, and Bill and I close behind. He walks slowly, deliberately, meticulously putting one foot solidly in front of the other, the message not getting through instantly. We are fearful.

As we walk, we sing—popular songs, camp songs, and country songs. Bill and Mike have beautiful voices, sweet and clear. Others can't sing so well, but it doesn't matter.

The children go on ahead checking out the trail. They climb boulders or examine vegetation. They don't want to get too far ahead of us. Then suddenly Andrea sings out, "Log down!" She and Matt wait until Bill gets there and very carefully lift each foot across the log. If the tree is really huge, Bill sits down on it and the kids swing his legs over. And we're on our way again until Matt calls out, "Trail blocked!" and Bill is helped over another obstacle. The birds warble, crickets chirp, and we sing our way through the forest. There are moments when I cannot sing.

On the trail we meet other hikers, who either laugh or applaud our singing or join in for a while, their voices growing dimmer as they move along the trail. At times we sit on a log and eat trail mix and drink water; then we're off again.

When I think about that day, it is not only about the courage it must have taken to start out through the forest. If Bill was fearful, and he surely must have been, he didn't show it. So I think instead about how he sang and smiled and the sheer joy he felt in being up on his feet walking, with all of us, in a place he loved.

It's Raining Again

We used to walk on city streets
in gentle summer rain.
It splashed on pewter sidewalks,
making happy little sounds
beneath our feet.
Rain dripping off his nose and chin
made us laugh.
On the old stone bridge
we made clown faces
in the rippling water below.
Gray skies enfolded us
in silver mist.
His laughing brown eyes
looked into mine.
He took my hand
and bending down
kissed me in the rain.
Now when the sound and scent
of summer rain
invades my senses,
I shut my door,
close my curtains,
turn on loud music,
and pretend I'm not so lonesome.

My Little Sister

"You have a baby sister!" my father whispered. "Wake up! You can come and see her now. Remember to be very quiet!"

I tiptoed into Martha's room where the little white iron bed had been temporarily set up. She looked so tiny wrapped up in a fluffy pink blanket. I held her perfect little hand and whispered, "I'm your big sister. Hurry up and get big so we can do stuff." I know she heard me. She kinda smiled.

But it wasn't all joy in our house that day because Mother was seriously ill. She had pneumonia. Two nurses had been installed in our house. They walked around silently caring for Mother. In their starched white uniforms and quiet white shoes, all of us children were intimidated and very much in awe.

My two older sisters, Martha and Lu, thirteen and fourteen, took over the complete care of the new baby. They took turns getting up at night to fix bottles and wash clothes.

After weeks of waiting for the fever to break, Dr. Hartford told us Mother was going to make it, but it would take many weeks for a full recovery.

They decided to name the baby Virginia. One of my father's good friends was Walter Lyons. His daughter, Virginia, just out of high school, needed a job. My father took her into his hardware store sort of as a training program. She did so well that he hired her full time. Dad became very fond of her and decided to name the baby after her, and Mary for Mother. Mary Virginia soon became Ginny.

When Ginny was almost two years old, I often took care of her. My cousin Millie, just my age, lived in a house two doors up from mine. For some reason I could never understand she had been given to her grandmother. Her own mother, father, sister, and two brothers lived in Pittsburgh. The grandparents were quite old and nothing exciting ever happened at their house so Millie spent most of her time at our house where there was never a dull moment.

Millie and I treated Ginny like a doll. We dressed her up and took her with us wherever we went. I'll admit sometimes we tried to get away without her. Before we'd get out of sight, we'd hear Mother calling, "Take Ginny with you!"

Ginny had beautiful little dresses with panties to match, that Mother made for her. Her favorite one was a yellow and white checked gingham dress with little chickens embroidered all around the bottom of the dress. Another one I remember was white dotted Swiss with blue flowers all around the neck and puff sleeves. She had a little black velvet coat with tiny pearl buttons. We'd dress her up in that coat and her small patent leather Mary Janes, her hair in a soft curl on top of her head, and show her off to our friends.

I made her a dress out of two red bandana handkerchiefs. I sewed it up the sides leaving room for her arms and tied knots on the shoulders. She loved that dress! Soon other kids were bringing handkerchiefs to be made into dresses, some pretty ratty looking.

She saw a pair of red shoes in a store window that she thought she just had to have. Dad thought it was ridiculous. I hunted up a pair of her old brown sandals and painted them with leftover red enamel. She was the envy of all the little girls in the neighborhood. Soon they were coming with old shoes to be painted. Red shoes really do run faster!

Ginny had a funny little bathing suit made of navy blue wool, with a red sailor collar, and a wide red stripe around her fat baby middle. She'd wear that bathing suit and a white rubber bathing cap trimmed with purple flowers. On a sun-washed afternoon she could play for hours in a tub of water in the back yard.

Once we lived in a very old small house. I think we were waiting on a larger house to become available. At any rate, Ginny and I were relegated to the attic where Mother had set up two cots side by side. The attic was unfinished. The only place you could stand up, without bumping into sloping ceilings, was in the center. It was miserably cold, no heat at all in the winter. On windy nights, snow drifted in through old windows. A light bulb on a long black cord hung over our beds.

Each night, bundled into our flannel pajamas, we'd open the door into the attic and race up the narrow stairs into the frigid air. I tucked the covers in around Ginny's cot like an envelope. Then she crawled in the top under lots of blankets, leaving hands free enough to hold a book. Then she'd giggle as I tried to struggle into my envelope. We could both read holding our books with half-covered hands.

She read *Winnie the Pooh*, while I studied Latin. Every few minutes she'd laugh and read aloud something funny that she wanted to share with me. To this day my mind can't seem to distinguish between Caesar and Winnie.

It all sounds like a hardship, but actually we made an adventure out of it. I remember it as one of the best times with her—all full of laughter.

Ginny had a little dog, a small short-haired white mutt, who followed us home one day. My father was not a dog lover. He refused to let her in the house. But he allowed Ginny to make a place for her in the basement which was warm and dry. Here Ginny made a bed for her with an old rug and a worn red quilt. She named the dog Carlo Mae Agnes. She loved that little dog! We took her with us on long walks on grass hills behind our house, where the grass grew tall and wildflowers filled the air with sweetness.

One day when Carlo Mae Agnes played in the backyard, a huge dog attacked her. She was all torn up, completely destroyed. Ginny carried her to her little bed and sat next to her all night until she died. Dad helped bury Carlo Mae Agnes in the backyard under the mulberry tree. She never had another dog until she married Phil.

By this time I was married to Bill and living in Slippery Rock, Pennsylvania. Ginny was a senior in high school, and she decided to come live with us. Martha brought all Ginny's clothes, many dresses and a fur coat, no less. In her beautiful clothes, her lovely green eyes, and her soft brown shoulder length hair, she took that little country school by storm.

Academically, well, that's another story, but she did manage to get the smartest boy in the whole school.

She and Phil were married shortly after graduation. They both became teachers.

One Summer

When I was eight years old, I spent one whole summer on a farm. My grandfather, who was a funeral director in town, owned a farm about five miles away.
He had a tenant farmer who shared the crops, took care of the animals, and was responsible for the farm.

Fred was the hired man. He had worked for Grandfather for years. He was loyal and reliable, but he wasn't capable of managing the farm. He came early each morning and left after the chores were finished in the evening.

In the middle of the night the tenant left. This left Grandfather with a serious problem. So he asked Mother if she would move to the farm for the summer. Mother, who would do most anything for her father, agreed.

So here we are! Mother and six kids, the oldest one twelve, the youngest just three. A small two-bedroom house, no electricity, no phone, no indoor bathroom, no car. Mother never learned to drive.

Dad owned a hardware store in town and came out to the farm several nights a week. When he worked late, he stayed in town. I don't think Dad liked the farm all that much. But to us kids it was the beginning of an adventure.

Fred milked the cows early in the morning, then brought the milk up to the spring house. The spring house? I'd never heard of such a thing. The spring house was a wonderful little house built underground. The door was only half visible, then down three steps, another door, and suddenly you're in a cool dark room.

"Why is it so cool? It's hot outside," Lu said.

"It's built over a spring that has cold clear water all year," Mother explained. Crocks were lined up against the wall. Mother and Fred filled them with the fresh milk.

"In the morning I'll skim the cream off the top and we'll make butter," Mother said.

I looked at Milt. He made a motion around his head that meant Mother must be crazy. We knew about butter. We bought it at the market all wrapped in wax paper and it wasn't in milk.

Next morning we went back to the spring house, and Mother skimmed the cream off the top of the crocks. We took it up to the kitchen, and Mother poured it into this big wooden thing she called a churn. She gave me a stick; she said it was a dasher.

"Now push that up and down inside the churn. Take turns, it will take a little while."

So we all took turns. It was pretty dumb, but Mother seemed to think it would make butter so we went along. I waited for her to say magic words.

Finally it got harder and harder to push that dasher.

"I think it's butter now," Mother said. She very carefully took the dasher out and the churn was full of beautiful golden lumps of butter. That's some kind of miracle.

We each picked our favorite tree in the orchard. I chose mine because Grandfather said it would have Grimes Golden apples, my favorite kind in the whole world. Also I could jump up and get the first limb and easily climb the tree. Milt and Jimmy could climb most any tree in the orchard. Marty got an easy one and Lu wouldn't even think of climbing a tree.

One thing I didn't like on the farm was the chickens. Those big brown chickens did nothing all day but amble around and eat. Then they'd finally get around to laying one egg, the only useful thing they ever did. They were so selfish they'd fight you tooth and nail if you took the egg. They'd peck your hands and your arms and squawk so loud you'd think they were being tortured. I've never seen any creature so selfish and mean-spirited.

Those chickens have a nice house with all their friends, if they are friends, and nests full of sweet smelling hay. Maybe they feel crowded, but they should see all of us up at that little house! I really hated those fat brown chickens!

One chicken was an exception. She was lighter in color, kind of golden brown. She followed Jimmy everywhere he went. He could pick her up and pet her. Jimmy named her Doris. She'd sit beside him on the porch and lay an egg, then hop down and leave it like a present. Doris was the only decent chicken I ever knew.

We all watched when Fred and his helper Joe sheared about one hundred sheep. They were hard to catch and weren't too happy about having all that wool cut off. But it must have felt better afterward because who wants to wear a big wool coat all summer? Sometimes after they were caught, they kicked and bleated so loud it filled the whole sheep barn.

Then one sheep, half sheared, just suddenly quit kicking and bleating and lay still.

"The heat was just too much for this one," Fred said. He laid it over on a pile of straw. "I'll take care of it later."

Marty started to cry and we all look scared and unhappy. This was something we'd never thought about before.

In the morning we went back to the barn to look at the dead sheep. It wasn't there. Perhaps Fred had already buried it.

Fred came into the barn laughing. "Look over there at the flock of sheep. See anything funny? She didn't die after all."

We looked and there was one sheep half sheared, one side snow white, the other side thick gray wool. Another miracle!

A beautiful collie dog came with the farm. From the first day Charlie loved that dog. Her name was Tango. Charlie was only three, half the size of the dog. In the morning he'd stand in the lane and call, "Here Tango, here Tango!" And the dog would run straight at Charlie and knock him down. Charlie would get up and all day they'd follow each other around. Next day the same thing, Charlie would call Tango and be knocked down again.

"You know she'll knock you down, Charlie," Mother said.

Charlie didn't care. Every morning that summer, he was out there calling, "Here Tango! Here Tango!" And every morning that dog joyously ran to a laughing Charlie and knocked him over.

Late in the summer when the apples were getting ripe, I climbed into my tree. Away up there I could sit among green leaves and eat a Grimes Golden apple. It's like no other taste in the world. A Grimes is not too sweet, not too tart, crisp and juicy. But it's not that. It's something different. To bite into a Grimes Golden apple is to taste warm summer days, bright sunshine, cool nights. It's green leaves, and birdsong, and drone of bees, and night sounds. I eat my Grimes Golden apple and dream away the day. Happiness is so easy!

One afternoon in late summer Dad came home early. It was unusual for him to come to the farm in the middle of the day.

"What's wrong? Are you sick? You look so tired," Mother was anxious.

"I don't feel well. I think I'll go up and lie down. Probably coming down with a cold or something."

When Mother checked on Dad a short while later, she was alarmed at the way he looked. He was so hot and had trouble breathing. He assured her he just needed to rest. At midnight he was much worse. Now he was thrashing about and talking wildly. Mother knew he had to have a doctor. It wasn't safe to wait until morning when Fred would come.

At the end of the lane, a quarter of a mile, the Failors had a telephone. She knew she couldn't leave Dad. Could she send one of the children in the middle of the night? She had no choice. But which one could go?

"Children, wake up, come down quickly! Don't waste a minute. One of you must go down to Failors and call Dr. Hartford to come immediately. Your father is very sick."

"Is Daddy going to die?" Jimmy was near tears.

"Of course not. The doctor can make him better."

"I'll go," Lu said, "I'm the oldest."

"I'll go with her," Marty said.

"I'm the oldest boy, I'll go. I'm not afraid of the dark," Milt said. "Me and Jimmy, we'll go, we can run fast."

Mother hesitated a moment, then made up her mind. "You'll all go! Now quickly, get dressed, wear shoes, a light jacket. Milt, you can carry the lantern. Now hurry!"

"I'm going," Charlie said.

"You can't go Charlie," I said. "Someone has to stay and help Mother. Can you do that?"

"I can do that. I'll help take care of Daddy."

"Now go," Mother said. "Walk as fast as you can, stay close together."

Milt went first carrying the lantern, Jimmy close behind him. Lu, Marty, and I followed close behind. The night was pitch black, the road ahead, we knew, was long and narrow. No moon, no lights anywhere except in the pale light of the lantern. The night air was cool, and deep hollows in the lane even colder. We walked as fast as we could. The world seemed so big and we were so alone.

"Will Daddy die if we don't get there in time?" Jimmy asked.

"We'll get there in time," I said. "Mother won't let him die."

I don't know if I believed it but the little sheep didn't die, and we made butter, and my tree grew apples, and the farm was full of miracles, and we must be halfway there, and so far safe, and I'm not scared, not very scared anyway, and he can't die, Mother couldn't live without Dad.

Suddenly Lu said, "I hear something!" We stopped, breathless, and waited. A slight rustling beside us, like someone walking through grass.

My heart was pounding so hard I could hardly breathe.

"I don't hear anything," Marty said. "Anyway we can't stop."

"There it is again! Listen!"

This time we all heard it. Someone was following us!

Milt lifted the lantern up as high as he could. Then he laughed. "It's Daisy, our cow. We're beside the pasture; she heard us and got up."

Minutes later all five of us were pounding on the door at the Failor's house.

"Daddy's gonna die if we don't get the doctor," Milt said.

"He's hot and he doesn't even know us!"

"We hurried all the way."

"The doctor's gonna make him better."

While Mrs. Failor tried to calm us down, Mr. Failor was already calling Dr. Hartford.

When he arrived, we all piled into his old Ford to go back up the lane. It didn't seem so long now and in no time at all we were home, and the doctor was taking care of my dad. He sat beside him all night working to bring the fever down. He had pneumonia; it took weeks before he was all well again.

On Dr. Hartford's last visit, he called all of us together. "You children did a very brave thing," he said. "A pitch black night can be scary for an adult. You saved your father's life. We're all proud of you."

"Me too," Charlie said. "Cause I helped Momma."

The Nickel

"You can go for a walk if you all stay together," Mother says. "Don't go any farther than the little store. When you get back it will be time for supper, and your father will be home."

When we are about to leave Mother calls out, "Take Julie with you, she should get out, and Marty, she'll need her little pink sweater. I don't want her to get sick again."

We troop out, all seven of us, four-year-old Julie holding tight to Marty's hand.

"I suppose we'll have potatoes again," Milt grumbles. "I'm sick of potatoes."

"Me too, potatoes, potatoes. I wish I'd never see another potato," Marty says.

"It's better than nothing. Maybe Mother will think of a new way to fix them," I say hopefully.

"Mother says some children don't even have potatoes," Lucy offers.

"They can have mine," Milt says. "Just pack them up and send them every last potato!"

"I like potatoes," Charlie says.

"You're just saying that, Charlie, cause you want to get on the good side of Mother. What do you know anyway? You're only five."

"I'm five, going on six and you can't say that." Charlie's blue eyes fill with tears.

"Don't cry, Charlie, Jimmy didn't really mean it," Lucy puts her arm around Charlie.

"Mr. Tony gave us a big basket of potatoes," Charlie holds his arms out wide. "And apples too. I love apples."

They struggle along, Milt leading the way. They can see into a house where a woman is carrying a platter of food. Several children sit ready to eat, a man smiles at the head of the table.

"I think they're having more than potatoes."

"Maybe their papa has a job."

"Mother says we need to get Papa's spirits up," Lucy says.

"What are spirits?" Charlie asks.

"I guess it's the way you feel."

"Like when you're hungry?"

"No, more inside yourself and the whole world is gray."

"If we say we like potatoes, will Papa's spirits come up?"

"It might help."

"Then would Papa find a job, and Mother wouldn't cry in her room any more?" asked Jimmy.

"We could try!"

We all agree except Julie. She's only four. I guess she doesn't understand about spirits.

Suddenly Jimmy lets out a shout, jumps up and down, whirls around, laughs and holds out his hand. "Look what I found—a nickel, a real nickel."

"I think it should belong to all of us. We're here together," Marty says.

"It's my nickel! I found it!"

"What are you going to do with it? Are you going into the little store?"

"Mother said not to go in," Lucy reminds us.

"But that's because we didn't have any money to spend. I guess we could go in now because I have my nickel."

We've been in the store with Mother. It's a wonderful place! The store is small and old and weathered to a pale gray. The steps have deep grooves from the shuffle of many feet. When Lucy opens the door, a little bell tinkles to tell Mr. Ciderman he has a customer. The wide floor boards have been oiled to a deep brown. Mr. Ciderman meets us at the door. He isn't pleased. "What are all you kids doing here? Where's your mother? If you aren't here to buy something, you have no reason to be here!"

"I have money." Jimmy holds up his nickel.

"Where did you get that?"

"I found it!"

"Where? Here in my store?"

"No, outside, on the way here. It's my nickel. I found it."

We go in as quietly as we can, sorta scared without Mother.

The store isn't crowded. Two women are standing over by the bread counter. One has beautiful dark hair held up with a bright comb. She smiles at us. The other woman is thin, with long stringy hair and a disgruntled unhappy face.

"Who are all these kids?" Smiling lady asks.

"Those are the Dolans! They rented that big old house on the corner. They needed it with that bunch!"

"They're all Dolans, all seven?"

"That's right, all seven. That's a disgrace! My one is trouble enough."

"They seem nice enough. They're just looking around."

"Father's out of work too. Bet he's sorry he has that crew."

"Lots of men are out of work now. He'll find something."

We head straight for the long glass case displaying candy. Momentous decisions to be made. So many choices! You can get two mothballs, pure white with a yummy almond in the center. There's a Clark bar that you can eat all the crunchy part and have a long strip of caramel to eat last.

"Get a Clark bar Jimmy. We could share that."

"I haven't decided."

There are jaw breakers. They're lots of fun. They are two for a nickel. You could get one now and take the other one home. They are so big you can hardly get on in your mouth at first. It changes colors and flavors so you can take it out of your mouth every few minutes to see what color it is. Or you can open your mouth and ask a friend. But I guess you couldn't share jaw breakers.

"How about a licorice stick Jimmy? We could share that."

"I haven't decided."

"Look at these Necco Sweets. They'd be easy to share."

"Maybe."

On the counter small green and brown paper bags stand in a neat row.

"What's in those?"

"That's popcorn, five cents, a good buy."

Mr. Ciderman picks up a bag and hands it to Jimmy. Jimmy shakes his head. "I haven't decided."

"Well make up your mind. I haven't got all day."

We move over to the other side of the store. In the corner there's a huge barrel full of dill pickles. I love the pungent smell of brine and dill. Tongs hang on the side of the barrel so you can fish out your own pickle.

"A pickle is a good choice, get the biggest one."

Jimmy hesitates, looks into the barrel, sniffs the delicious briny smell then moves reluctantly to another counter where there's a great round of yellow cheese. Mr. Ciderman is wearing a white apron and waving a big knife.

"I'll cut off a nice piece of cheese for you, just a nickel."

"We could share that," Marty says.

"I haven't decided."

Hanging above the counter there are strings of purple onions and a rope of pale garlic. Of course he wouldn't want to buy those but they're beautiful, just hanging there. All the smells and sounds and colors mingled together are pertinent to only one place—Ciderman's little store.

Jimmy wanders back to the pickle barrel, picks up the tongs, hesitates, then slowly and deliberately places them back on the barrel.

"I've decided," he says. He walks over to the refrigerator counter.

"I'll take a carton of milk please." He takes the nickel out of his pocket and hands it to Mr. Ciderman.

"Milk! You want milk?"

"Yes please, and a straw."

"You don't need a straw. You're a big boy. You can drink right out of the carton."

"Is the straw free?"

"Of course it's free."

"I'll take a straw please."

He picks up the carton of milk, carefully opens the top, places the straw in the proper place, and hands the milk to Julie.

As she puts the straw in her mouth and takes that first drink of cold, sweet, wonderful milk, her blue eyes are shining stars.

Then those Dolan kids leave the store and head for home.

Round About the Neighborhood

At the end of our street where the sidewalk ends and turns into the dirt road, that is where the Taggerts live. They are the third generation of Taggerts to live here. The house is set way back from the road, a large white colonial with tall pillars and a wide front porch. It is backed by wooded hills. On one side of a winding road, there's a large pond surrounded by weeping willows, on the other side a sweep of perfectly manicured lawn.

Mr. Taggert lives here with his wife and three daughters.

We liked to walk out past the Taggert's house because it was not only beautiful, but was exciting and dangerous. It was like walking in the cemetery at night. You knew you'd be scared half out of your wits. I don't think we really believed that dead people rise up out of their graves and chase you. Still, you never can tell. Other kids said it happened to them. We were always willing to take a chance.

That's the way it was with the Taggerts. If you so much as stepped a foot on Mr. Taggert's lawn, he would get his rifle and shoot you. You had to be very careful as you walked by. You wouldn't dare make a wrong move. What if you got into an argument with the boys and Jimmy pushed you and you accidentally fell into Taggert's yard! You'd be shot in the back, right there and the kids would have to drag you home. It's not worth thinking about what Dad would say!

So we walk very, very carefully in the middle of the sidewalk. Some kids were afraid to go near Taggerts.

Perhaps we wanted to show off, but to us, it was exciting and adventurous to go just as near as we could to danger.

The windows seemed to have eyes, and behind each window, we wondered, if Mr. Taggert stood there with his rifle ready, just waiting for one of us to make a misstep. One day he came out on the porch. We were too scared to run, just walked stiffly along, hearts racing, feet almost refusing to move.

I never knew of anyone who actually got shot. But you would have to be pretty stupid to try and prove it. And we were pretty smart kids, yeah, you couldn't fool us!

People said Mr. Taggert wanted to protect his daughters from the local boys. But I had seen Mr. Taggert's daughters, and I didn't believe there was any reason to think the fellows were going to be exactly storming the doors!

So whenever things got dull at home someone would say, "Let's go out to Taggerts."

So far none of us ever got shot.

The Pond

We lived in this big old white house, all nine of us. My father bought it from Mr. Cohen because it had six bedrooms and Dad said it had potential. I thought it was just fine the way it was, but he decided to have it completely remodeled.

The men who came to do it over weren't too happy with seven kids underfoot so Dad decided to move us all to a little house he owned just on the edge of town, until the big house was ready for us.

The little house wasn't too bad, kinda fun in fact. One thing that made it all worthwhile was Hammy Marks, a curly haired boy who lived across the street. He rode past on his bicycle several times a day. I think his attention was all on Lu, my oldest sister, who was twelve and really pretty. But Marty and I could pretend, couldn't we?

The large lot next to our little house was just a bare old field, not a tree or a bush on it. Dad said it was off limits.

The weather had been dry and hot for days. Everyone was hoping for rain. Reverend Jacobson, at our Methodist Church, was praying for rain. God must have heard him because it started to rain the very next day. At first it was just a sprinkle; then it turned into a real downpour. Lightning and thunder filled the air. The windows in the little house rattled and it was hard to get to sleep. It rained all night.

In the morning the first thing I noticed was silence. I know you can't actually hear silence. But in a way you can. You know it's there. It's all around you like a soft blanket. I just lay there too contented to move.

Finally I decided to get up and look out the window to see what damage the storm had done. Something was terribly wrong! Was I half asleep and dreaming! There beside our house was a pond, not just a puddle but a real pond. I thought Dad must have moved us during the night. He probably decided the place was too little after all. But how could he do that? I ran to another window. There was Hammy Marks' house. Another window, Mrs. Nausbaum on her porch. I wakened my brothers and sisters. We all crowded around the window looking at the new pond.

"There wasn't a pond there yesterday," Marty said.

"Who brought us the pond?" Jimmy said.

"I think the rain must have made the pond," Lu said.

"Reverend Jacobson prayed too hard, didn't he?"

I opened the window so we could see better. The air was filled with loud croaking.

"Frogs! Our pond is full of frogs."

"How did they get here?"

"Somebody brought them in the night. Someone who had too many."

"In a truck maybe, or in a wagon?"

"Maybe Reverend Jacobson prayed for the frogs."

"That's silly! Why would he want frogs!"

"Let's get dressed and go out and see how many they brought," Milt said.

We stood wide-eyed beside our pond. Hundreds of happy, croaking frogs, leaping about, glad to be in their new place.

Suddenly Milt said, "I have a wonderful idea. I bet we could get rich. I bet we could make lots of money, maybe even a hundred dollars!" Milt was always thinking up ways to get rich.

"Nobody's gonna buy frogs," Marty said.

"You're crazy Milt!"

"No, really, I heard Mr. Merwin telling Dad that if he wanted a real good meal to go down to Fast Freddy's All You Can Eat where you can get frog legs. He said it was better than chicken."

"How are we gonna get the frogs down there?"

"We'll have to catch them, put them in a bucket."

"I think we better wait until Dad goes to the store," Lu said.

"What about Mother?" Marty asked.

"Today's the day she goes to Fancy Work Club," I remembered.

"Mrs. Nausbaum will come to baby-sit, but she listens to the radio and goes to sleep when baby Ginny takes her nap. We'll promise not to go out of the yard."

"Let's go in and eat breakfast with Dad first."

We didn't mention the new pond. We ate cornflakes and drank our orange juice without complaining. Dad was in a good mood.

Mother came down to say goodbye before she left for Fancy Work Club. She'd be gone for several hours. She was wearing her beautiful pink blouse with lots of lace. And her real pearls that Dad gave her for her birthday. She's the prettiest mother in our whole town, maybe in the whole world.

Mrs. Nausbaum arrived and got busy with Ginny and the radio and a new romance book. We were safe.

Now we had to decide things. Jimmy, Milt, Marty, and I would wade into the pond and catch frogs. Lu, who didn't want to go into the water, was to be the secretary. She would count the frogs as they were brought out of the pond. She'd need a table, some paper and a pencil. Jimmy volunteered to go into the house and get a small table from the living room and mother's address book. There were pages in the back of the book never even used. That and a pencil and Lu was all set to be the secretary.

"I want to catch frogs," Charlie said.

Charlie, only three years old, was way too little to catch frogs.

"I'll find a job for you Charlie," I said.

"Where do we put the frogs?" Marty asked.

"We'll put them in the wash tub. I'll get it out of the basement."

"That will be your job, Charlie, a very important job, to keep the frogs from jumping out of the tub."

We waded into the pond. We didn't think it would be so deep, but we were up to our waists in squishy, cool mud. The frogs were easy to catch, you could even get two at a time. There were frogs everywhere, laughing and croaking. We kept bringing them out, putting them in the tub.

"They're jumping out!" Charlie yelled.

"We need something on top of the tub."

"I'll get the screen off the kitchen window," Jimmy said.

With the screen on the tub Charlie was able to keep most of the frogs from getting out.

"How many, Lu?"

"So far seventy-five," Lu reported.

"We're gonna be rich!"

We didn't realize how long we'd been catching frogs. When you're making money that fast, you don't think about the time.

Suddenly, right there beside the pond was Dad. He didn't say a word for the longest time. Just stood there in his blue suit, his white shirt, and his blue striped tie.

Then in a quiet, very quiet voice he said, "What-in-the-name-of-God-are-you-doing!"

His hands were down at his sides, clenched into fists. I never saw him like that. I wanted him to yell.

"We're gonna sell the frogs to Fast Freddy's All You Can, better than chicken," Milt said.

"We're gonna be rich," Jimmy said.

"We have one hundred frogs already!" Lu said.

Dad shouted, "I don't want to hear another word, not *one word*. Now get all those frogs back in the water, everyone of them. NOW!"

We didn't waste any time.

"Get up here. Let me look at you."

We stood in a row, covered with black, smelly muck. Charlie's big blue eyes were full of tears. He'd never seen Dad like this. Dad was never angry at Charlie.

"You're all filthy! Go down to the basement and hose yourselves off. Leave your clothes down there. Then come up to the kitchen."

In our dirty underwear, with the worst of the mud off, we waited for Dad. What would he do to us? We'd probably be grounded for a year.

"Now," Dad said, "Go upstairs, get baths, and get into your pajamas. And stay there!"

After our baths we all huddled into one room.

"Do you think we'll get any supper?" Jimmy said.

"And tonight's macaroni and cheese," Marty said sadly.

"I'm so hungry!" Charlie said.

"Maybe Mother will bring us some bread and butter," I said.

Now we could smell pork chops and macaroni and cheese. I thought about Mother and Dad sitting there at the big dining room table eating and never thinking about us.

Then Mother called, "Children, dinner is ready! Come on down!"

We went down, quietly, carefully, and took our places at the table.

Mother was still in her beautiful clothes, but now with a white apron tied around her waist. She seemed to have a cold because every once in a while she'd start to cough and have to put her hand up and cover her mouth. Each time Dad would frown a little. He didn't look at Mother.

For a long time after that nobody mentioned frogs.

We often ate at Fast Freddy's All You Can Eat. I never ordered frog legs, better than chicken.

We finally moved back into our beautiful big house.

Hammy Marks continued to be our friend.

We never got rich.

Fourth of July Fireworks

You hear a lot of talk nowadays about a safe and sane Fourth of July. I quite agree. That's just as it should be. But for sheer excitement, I'll never forget one Fourth when I was about nine years old. We had fireworks to end all fireworks.

My father decided that year to put all the money into a night display. No noisemakers at all.

We left for my grandmother's early on the morning of the Fourth. My mother thought it might rain before we got back, so my brother and I took our brand new raincoats. We folded them very carefully over a huge bundle containing the fireworks.

At my grandmother's all the cousins had arrived. Everyone was excited. My father brought in the bundle, the raincoats still on top, amid squeals of delight at its unusual size. He placed it cautiously on the back porch with a warning that no one, absolutely no one, was to touch anything until dark.

We picnicked and played games and had contests all day. Between events we made trips to the back porch and peeked under the raincoats at the fabulous package.

By six o'clock we were asking when we could start shooting things off. My father kept telling us to wait. All the grownups were talking together in the house and our impatience was almost more than we could bear.

We waited. Then asked again, and again we waited. By this time it was dusk, and I decided just one sparkler couldn't possibly do any harm. All the cousins quickly agreed. We were breathless with expectancy.

I very carefully took one sparkler off the top of the pile. My brother supplied a match. It didn't seem to light very easily. He tried again. Suddenly it flared up quickly. In my excitement I dropped it.

Everything began to happen at once. Colored flares lit up the dark sky like magic. Sparklers all sparkled at once. Sky rockets shot off that porch like mad and showers of sparks made unbelievable patterns in the night. Weird lights glowed on excited faces. Roman candles shot into the darkness, died down, made a funny pfft...pfft sound and shot off again. Pinwheels spun madly around in crazy circles, leaving a fantastic trail of colors. Children squealed in delight and fear and grownups shouted.

Aunt Bess went after things with a broom and my uncle tried his felt hat on the conflagration. It was dangerous and awful and quite wonderful.

Then suddenly it was over. The whole show plus two new raincoats had gone up in smoke in less than fifteen minutes. But I'll tell you, if I live to be a hundred*, I'll never see such a display of fireworks again.

*Editor's note: Wilma lived to be one hundred and one.

School Clothes Needing Alterations in September

Twice a year, the sewing lady came to our house—two weeks in September and again in May. Tine was a distant cousin of Mother's and made her entire living as a seamstress. She was a very good one who chose her families very carefully so we were fortunate to get her services twice a year.

Tine was a strikingly handsome woman who wore her dark hair pulled back loosely and fastened with a bright comb. Her sparkling brown eyes always seemed to be on the verge of laughter. During the daytime she wore a dark skirt and a plain snow-white blouse, but before dinner each evening she would change into a lovely pastel blouse and fasten an unusual pin on her collar.

All the clothes from the past season were tried on before she arrived so Mother could ascertain whether they could be made to fit by either lengthening, shortening, or remaking. I would watch anxiously as my older sisters tried their clothes on, hoping they could wear them another year. Otherwise I'd get them as hand-me-downs.

Mother had collected pieces of material, patterns, thread, buttons, and an assortment of trimming of all kinds. The new material was displayed on the dining room table and together Mother, Tine, and my sisters and I would decide how it was to be divided. My stack of clothes was already so high that I knew I didn't have a chance of getting many new ones. Martha, my sister, needed all new clothes because she always seemed to be outgrowing hers. As each piece of material was designated for her, she'd give me a "I don't wear hand-me-downs" smirk on her face.

One fall we all had beautiful middies. Martha's was green with darker green trim, mine was red trimmed in black, and Lu's was dark blue with gold trim. The next year I got all three and was so sick of wearing middies I never wanted to see one again.

The seamstress started sewing right after breakfast and kept at it all day long taking only a short time out for lunch. Mother helped when she could and enjoyed herself because she and Tine were good friends and had a lot to talk about.

They started on pajamas for the boys and then little suits for Charlie who was two. Lu was the oldest so she was next in line. She liked trying on each dress when it was in the process of being made. Her wardrobe usually included one or two good dresses for Sunday and special occasions, a couple others for school, and finally an assortment of skirts, jumpers, and blouses.

When it was Martha's turn, she refused to try them on when Tine asked her. Instead she flounced around and carried on something fierce, even hiding at times. Mother threatened to give all her clothes to me and that usually set her straight.

To be honest I didn't blame her because I didn't like standing there in the dining room in my underwear, either. How did we know who might suddenly come into the room while Tine was pinning and measuring and we were standing still? What if a boy from the second grade came past the house and saw me standing there in my underwear? I'd have to quit school!

Although I didn't need any new clothes, Mother always saw to it that I got one beautiful dress and a few new blouses. I remember one dress; I must have been seven years old. It was powder blue silk crepe, long-waisted and had a wide red sash in the back with a huge bow. I loved that dress because I felt like a princess when I wore it.

In the evenings after dinner, Dad usually took us for a ride in the Studebaker. Mother sat in the front with Dad, Tine and we girls in back, and the boys were on the little pull-up seats in the middle. We sang silly songs and made up sillier riddles. Dad would pretend that he had to hurry back home, but he always stopped for ice cream.

When all the sewing was finished and we were ready for the new school year, we drove Tine to her home just over Ohio's state line. It was a rambling white house with green shutters and a wraparound porch where she lived with her sisters. They served chicken and dumplings to us on their oak kitchen table.

The sewing lady and hand-me-down clothes are a bit of Americana that I'll always remember.

My Sister Martha

It was prom night for my sister Martha. First the prom, followed by graduation, then a wonderful life with Walter.

Martha had been going with Walter since Junior High School. He was like part of our family. They planned to get married after she graduated from nurse's training. She had always wanted to be a nurse, but recently she and Walter decided they wanted to be married soon after graduation. They had been discussing it for days with our parents.

"Don't you think it would be better if you got your training first?" Mother asked. "That way you'd be prepared to earn a living."

"I won't need to. Walter has a good job working with his father."

"What is the hurry?" Dad asked. "Walter will wait for you."

"But we don't want to wait! You don't understand! We want to be together now."

"Let's talk more about it later," Mother suggested.

Martha is the conductor of the high school orchestra. Once a month we have assembly in the auditorium. No matter how much we dislike school, assembly is a real break. We march in, subdued, quiet, bored. We take our seats and wait for Mr. Higgins. When he enters the room, we all stand, like he's royalty or something. It's hard not to laugh. He's short, and his clothes hang loosely on him. His gray hair is combed kinda sideways to cover the bald spot (as if). He is wearing his usual red bow tie, small black rimmed glasses. He looks a bit like Barney Fife. We stand at attention.

"Good morning!" he says. "You may be seated."

Then he tells us we're the best class he's ever had, he's proud of us. We're all going to do great things—keep up the good work! Same old, same old. He signals to Martha and the orchestra breaks into a rousing song. Now things are looking up! We sing a couple of songs. *Always* and *Let You Call Me Sweetheart.* Nothing old hat about Mr. Higgins.

Edwin plays the piano, Kenneth the violin, and Martha and Walter sing beautifully together. Edwin can play anything you ask for, just hum it and he can play it. Kenneth joins right in. The four of them have been best friends since grade school. They come to our house so many times and play the best songs! Many times I lie in bed and listen to the music and the laughter and dream my own dreams.

When the last notes die down, Mr. Higgins says, "Now, Max, how about a few cheers!"

Max, a tall pretty girl with a crop of curly red hair, runs to the front of the room. Everybody loves Max. We all cheer and clap.

She leads us in one cheer after another. She runs lightly around the room, getting everyone involved. We're in a frenzy of excitement. Max can do that to you, and I don't even like sports! She puts her whole heart and soul into it.

"One, two, three, four! Who you gonna root for!" she yells.

"E-P-H-S!" we scream.

"Who?" she yells.

"E-P-H-S!" (louder.)

"Who?" she puts both hands up to her ears.

"E-P-H-S!" (we shake the rafters.)

There's enough energy in that room to make bright the whole town. Mr. Higgins signals Martha and the orchestra goes right into the *Washington Post March*. We settle down, happy and exhausted. Mr. Higgins waves his arms, a signal we're dismissed. Row by row we march out, exhausted and happy. How we love our school, we love our teachers, we even love Mr. Higgins. All the world is just waiting for us.

The four friends, Kenneth, Edwin, Martha, and Walter, gather up the music, put the chairs away. They are aware that this is the last time they'll play in the high school orchestra. But friendship is forever. They leave the auditorium laughing, Walter with his arm around Martha.

Annabella! How can I explain Annabella? She transferred to our school from Chicago for her senior year. In our town her clothes seem outrageous. Instead of penny loafers, she wears high heels, instead of skirts and blouses, she wears fancy dresses, too tight and too short with lots of fabulous jewelry. She looks at us, the girls, as if we just got off the turnip truck. She flirts with the boys who are totally mesmerized. Annabella never goes out with any of the high school boys. She finds older partners outside of our school. One good thing, Annabella can't go to the prom because you aren't allowed to go with anyone outside of our school.

Now it's all about the prom! Mother took Martha to Kaufman's in Pittsburgh to buy her prom dress. I got to go along. She wasn't sure just what she wanted except it had to be blue, blue like a summer sky, the color Walter wanted. She found the perfect dress, sky blue, delicate, shimmering, the stuff of dreams.

Mother took us up to the seventh floor to the restaurant in Kaufman's. It was like a world apart. White linen tablecloths, tall waiters in white coats, silver and crystal. A far cry from Homer's Homecooking All You Can Eat in our town. I don't remember what I ate. It was too exciting, a magic day.

Now finally it's time for the prom. Martha is ready. In her fabulous dress, with her bright curly hair, her very blue eyes, she's radiant with happiness. Mother places a fine gold chain with a single diamond around her neck, a touch of cologne.

She decides to wait upstairs by herself until Walter arrives. She wonders what kind of corsage he'll bring. She knows he will look handsome in his tux. Oh, she loves him so much! After graduation she and Walter will never be separated. They'll grow old together.

It's 8:15. Mother comes upstairs, Martha has begun to worry.

"Maybe he's having trouble getting dressed," Mother says. "I'm sure he'll be along any minute."

"His dad will help him," Mother says.

"Maybe it's car trouble. Just relax, Dear."

"It's 8:30," Mother says. "Do you want me to call his mother?"

"No, he wouldn't want me to check up on him. I'll just wait."

"Nine o'clock, I think I should call his parents. He may have had an accident."

She came back a few minutes later. She looks frightened.

"His mother said he went to the prom at 8:00," she said.

Mother doesn't say a word. Her face is pale, her eyes vacant. I stand beside her, take her hand. She doesn't know I'm there; I start to cry. Martha takes off her blue dress, folds it carefully and places it in the chest at the foot of her bed, removes her silver slippers, wraps them in tissue paper, places them beside her dress. She takes off the gold chain with the single diamond, puts it in a small box, lays it on top of the dress, closes the chest.

In a small voice, not Martha's voice at all, she says, "I want to be alone now."

Mother is distressed, her voice falters. "But Martha …"

"I'm all right, Mother. I'd rather be by myself."

"Can I send your father up?"

"No, just go."

In the middle of the night she cries, such an outpouring of profound grief, it's to break your heart.

In the morning Kenneth and Edwin come. They are distraught.

"We're so sorry, Martha. I'm sure Walter is ashamed. I know he loves you."

"He took Annabella! It's her fault, not Walter's!" Edwin says.

"Walter will come over, he's scared now. He knows he did an unspeakable thing." Kenneth takes her hand. She seems not to notice.

"It's all right. Thank you for coming. I'll be OK; not to worry." She smiles, but her eyes are haunted and full of deep sadness.

The next morning Martha packed her clothes. Said good-bye to her family, and left for nurse's training.

She became a very fine nurse. She was especially good with children, singing to them, telling them stories, while she took good care of them.

When Martha was forty years old, she married John. I think she loved him. I'm sure she had a few happy years with him. She died when she was in her fifties.

But as long as she was alive in the world, a part of her was Walter's.

Grandfather

I never could understand how my grandfather ended up in a small town in Ohio. He came over from Ireland at the age of twenty-two.

Perhaps on his way west he stopped there and for some reason had to stay over for a few days. There was nothing to recommend the town, not a river, a lake, a scenic hill, or a valley. Just plain flat land and small meager farms.

Maybe he learned from a traveler that in this town and in all towns around, there wasn't a single undertaker. So he stayed and never left. He was soon to learn that the people were honest, hard-working, and appreciative of his Irish sense of humor.

He must have been quite a shock to the rather staid people of this small village. A wild Irishman, black curly hair, a beautiful face, and penetrating blue eyes that I've seen only in pictures. When I knew Grandfather, he had gray hair and a long beard.

He had a fiery Irish temper when he was unjustly provoked, but was kind and gentle to grieving families. When a man couldn't pay for the funeral of his wife, Grandfather told him not to worry, he'd take care of it. Later the man brought a four-poster bed in payment. A heartbroken mother, who couldn't pay to bury her baby boy, paid with a violin.

When he had been there about a year, he met and married my grandmother, Luella Conkle, a very proper, intellectual German girl. It seemed like an unlikely union but it was just what Grandfather needed. If he had a bad day, she was there to quietly sympathize. Evenings when he danced a jig, played the Jew's harp, sang *Old Dan Tucker* or *Danny Boy*, she joined right in with the family and the town's people.

Grandmother set a fine table. On weekdays it was everyday linen and stoneware china, on Sundays the good linen and Havelin china. She was always glad to set an extra plate for a grandchild or any random person that Grandfather brought in at the last minute. It could be one of his workers or a hungry man just passing through.

He built a fine, most unimposing house on Main Street. It was painted light brown with dark brown trim on long narrow windows. The ten-room house was heated with a fireplace in the downstairs rooms. Upstairs in winter you almost froze until you could get under the feather tick. There was a bathroom with running water and a very small gas stove that gave off a meager amount of heat. It was just in and out of there in a flash! A bath in the small tub, even with warm water, took a great deal of courage.

A wonderful banister came from upstairs. A curve at the bottom prevented you from falling off. Steps were for grownups.

There were three porches, a long narrow one across the front, just wide enough for a chair. On the side there was a tiny porch about five feet square. I thought it was just built for kids. You could play all sorts of games there. It could be a stage, a hideout, a store, or just a place to sit and read and dream.

On the back, off the kitchen, there's a big square porch with wooden benches along the side. Here you could sit and husk corn, peel apples, or crack walnuts. Grandmother could wash clothes out there or just sit and rest with a second cup of coffee.

From the back porch a long path led out to the barn where Blueridge, the riding horse, and Danny, the little brown pony, lived.

The house is still there, with a plaque near the front door, a registered historical home. The barn is long gone.

A few miles out of town Grandfather bought one hundred fifty acres, built a small house, stocked the farm with animals, and hired a tenant farmer.

Every morning, promptly at eight, Grandfather arrived at the barbershop for a shave. He was the first one, a very busy important person. One morning he had to wait; he swore he would never shave again. He never did.

On summer days when there isn't a funeral, Grandfather hitches Blueridge to the buggy and heads for the farm. He believes cars are just a fad. He always allows one of us to go along. We take turns, my two brothers and I.

I feel so important riding up high in the buggy. I'm aware of every rut, every stone, in the dusty brown road. I like the sound of Blueridge as he clip clops along and swishes his beautiful long tail.

Cars whiz by. They wave and call a greeting. They all know Grandfather. He has buried a friend or relative of everyone in town.

We arrive at the farm, and Grandfather unhitches Blueridge so he can eat grass and play while I have to work.

"What do you want me to do?" I ask. I know that part of the day I'm supposed to help.

"You can weed the vegetable garden."

"I hate weeding."

"Think of all the good eating you'll have come winter," he says.

"Like turnips and parsnips!" I grumble.

"How about a good mess of green beans with onions and bits of bacon?"

"OK. That's better. I'll weed the beans."

By noon I'm so hungry I can't wait for lunch.

"What are we having?" I ask Grandfather.

"Whatever Lu put up for us. It'll be good; you can count on that."

We sit beside the barn under the old elm tree. He has a blue enamel pail. It has two parts. In the top, thick slices of homemade bread filled with tender pink ham. Best of all, apple pie!

"Let's save our pie till last. What's in the bottom?"

"Warm sweet tea." We drink it out of the tin cups.

"Now it's time for the pie! It smells so good. Doesn't it smell just wonderful, Grandfather?"

"It sure does. You can't beat Lu' s pie. Here now, pick it up in your hands."

Oh the apples, the cinnamon, the butter!

We sit contentedly, Grandfather and I, savoring the moments.

"Now wash your hands at the pump and you can play for a while. I'll call you when it's time to go home."

Now I'm free to ride Sadie the work horse, climb trees, annoy the pigs, chase the chickens, or play with the new lambs. Afternoon is all too short.

Driving home, Blueridge pulls the buggy slowly. I seem so close to everything. The trees overhead form a cool green bower. Evening sunlight filters through the leaves making patterns on the road and on my hands. High up in the buggy, I lean on Grandfather.

Late one night he comes in from the barn. He is wearing a worn leather jacket, a Daniel Boone hat, and carries a kerosene lantern. It sways back and forth precariously, making weird shadows on the trees and on the worn stones of the walk.

The way from the barn is not long, but Grandfather slips on that perilous path and breaks his hip.

"Damnation!" he yells.

He spends the next ten years in a wheelchair. He lives with us. He's part of the family.

"How are things at the store?" he asks my father.

"Pretty good. Sales are up this week. Have a bit of trouble with some barn equipment, but I think it will work out."

"Can you hold Johnny while I set the table?" Luanne plops the baby onto Grandfather's lap.

"Learning to be a nurse is too hard," Marty complains. "I'm gonna quit!"

"You can't do that. Remember when you said you could never learn to ride a horse?"

"Yeah," Marty laughs. "After I fell off about a dozen times."

He listens to Jim and Milt argue about girls, just shakes his head.

He helps Charlie with his homework. Long division is hard!

He reads *Snowbound* with me on quiet evenings.

He plays checkers with Ginny and tells her tales of blue lakes, and bogs, and castles, thatched cottages, and lovely Connemara. Burning logs cast a rosy glow on Grandfather and my little sister.

"Get me one of those big Northern Spy apples over there. I'll peel it for you."

He takes a small knife out of his pocket. "Now watch! We want one long piece. It mustn't break!"

His slender fingers peel carefully, round and round. Ginny watches breathlessly. "You did it, Grandpa!"

She places it on glowing coals. Autumn fills the air.

"You think I need a haircut?" he asks me.

"You sure could use one."

"Get the scissors then."

"Who, me? I'm no barber! What do I know about cutting hair?"

"You can learn. Get the scissors."

"I'm no barber."

"Get a mirror. Now, a little off the top, and on the sides."

"You'll be sorry! You'll look like a skinned rat."

"Now trim my beard."

"Whata I know about beards? I'm no barber."

I cut his hair and trim his beard for the next ten years.

"Do you want to go to the movies, Grandfather? It's about horses."

"It's a bother with this chair."

"No bother, I want to see it too."

I push the wheelchair five blocks over rough streets and shove it into the back of the small town movie house. It smells of popcorn, mice, and sweaty kids.

We watch spirited Irish horses frolic over rolling emerald fields.

I look at Grandfather. Tears from his faded blue eyes stain his beautiful old face, brown and withered as leaves in autumn. Is he dreaming of that wild Irish boy who romped over lush green meadows in County Donegal?

I guide him home to security and smothered dreams.

He likes quiet time with my mother, his Mary. His first born. He helps her in the kitchen, creaming butter and sugar, cracking nuts, greasing pans. He eats soft fat ginger cookies, warm from the oven, drinks cold milk from a thick blue mug. They don't talk very much, they don't need to. The room is as thick with love as the yellow butter.

That's all so long ago! I miss him.

Grandfather's World

Grandfather was an undertaker,
He made heaps of money.
Had a fine house,
fine horses.
A more loving husband
and generous father,
You would never find.
He was a pushover
for his grandchildren,
Showed his fiery Irish temper
when unjustly provoked,
But was sweet and gentle
to the bereaved.

When a man couldn't pay
for a funeral,
It didn't bother Grandfather.
Years later
the man brought a four-poster bed
in payment.
A heartbroken mother
paid for her baby's funeral
with her violin.
Grandfather gave it to me
when I was ten.

Every morning
promptly at eight

Grandfather entered the barber shop.
He was an important man-
The town undertaker!
Always first for a shave.
One morning he had to wait,
Swore he'd never shave again
Never did.

On summer days, when there are no funerals
Grandfather hitches Blueridge
to the buggy and
heads for the farm.
(He believes cars are just a fad).
He takes one of us along,
Usually one of the boys.
But I get my turn!
I feel so important-
Riding up high in the buggy-
Aware of every rut, every stone
in the chocolate brown road.
Blueridge clops clops along
swishes his beautiful tail
to keep the flies off.

Cars whiz by,
People call greetings.
Everyone knows Grandfather.
He has buried a friend or relative
of everyone in town.
Today he is just Grandfather
And it's my turn.

At the farm we help the tenant farmer
Plant or weed, pick vegetables,

or feed the animals.
At noon we sit side by side
under the apple tree beside the barn.
Grandfather opens
his blue enamel dinner pail.
The top half holds sandwiches,
Tender pink ham between
thick slices of homemade bread.
Best of all, cold apple pie,
sweet, juicy, cinnamony,
To eat with sticky hands.
In the bottom of the pail
warm sweet tea.
He fills two tin cups.
We sit contentedly,
Grandfather and I,
Savoring the moments.

Lunch over, I am free to explore,
to ride Sadie the work horse,
Climb trees, play with the new lambs,
Chase the chickens, and annoy the pigs.
Until Grandfather calls me.
It's time to go home.

Driving home at dusk
The horse pulls the buggy
SLOWLY.
I seem so close to everything.
The trees meet overhead
forming a cool green bower.
Evening sunlight
filters through the leaves
Making patterns on the road

and on my hands.
High up in the buggy
I lean on Grandfather.

Late one night
Grandfather comes in from the barn.
He wears a worn leather jacket
a Daniel Boone hat,
carries a kerosene lantern
swaying back and forth
precariously,
making weird shadows
on glistening trees,
Lighting dimly the short way home.
Grandfather slips on that perilous path,
breaks a hip.
DAMNATION!
He doesn't believe in doctors-
spends his last ten years
In a wheelchair.

Grandfather needs quiet times
with my mother,
his Mary – his first born.
He helps her in the kitchen
creaming butter and sugar,
cracking nuts, greasing pans.
He eats soft, fat ginger cookies,
drinks cold milk from a thick blue mug.
He doesn't say much,
doesn't need to.
The room is as thick with love
As the yellow butter.

I take Grandfather to a movie.
I'm sure he'll like it.
It's a movie about horses.
I push the wheelchair five blocks over rough
    streets,
and shove the chair into the back
of the small town movie house.
It smells of popcorn and mice and
sweaty kids.
We watch spirited Irish horses frolic
on rolling emerald hills
in County Donegal,
I look at Grandfather.
Tears from his faded blue eyes
stain his beautiful old face,
brown and withered as leaves in autumn.
Is he dreaming of that wild Irish boy
who romped over lush green fields
in County Donegal?
I guide him home,
To security and smothered dreams.

Burning logs
Cast a rosy glow on Grandfather
and my little sister.
He peels a winter apple
a Northern Spy,
with a small knife
he takes from his pocket.
My little sister watches breathlessly
as his slender fingers
peel carefully, round and round-
One long piece.
It mustn't break.

She holds it up, triumphantly!
places it on glowing coals,
Autumn fills the air.

Grandfather, this gentle man,
whose life is in this house,
in these small rooms,
shares our joys, our frustrations,
and enriched all our lives.

The Train Trip

I'm going on a trip with my father. I've never been on a train before. I'm going from East Palestine, Ohio to Salineville, Ohio. I'm four years old and it's 1916.

I remember exactly what I was wearing, a brown coat with a small cape over the shoulders trimmed with white fur, a bonnet with the same white fur around my face. My prized possession was my fur muff and inside it a little pocket where I kept several pennies for Sunday School. My white boots kept my feet toasty warm.

As we stood waiting for the big black train to come roaring into the station, I wasn't scared one bit because my father was holding my small hand in his good strong one. He lifted me onto the train and we found a seat near the front. As soon as we got on our way, a tall brown man came up beside us. He was displaying all kinds of very small toys on his vest.

"Hello, Little Lady. Is this your first trip?"

"I love your train! But, are you burnt?"

"Hush, Billy."

When he stopped laughing, he said, "Oh, that's all right. I was born this way and we're called black."

"Can I touch your skin?" I asked.

I put my white hand on his smooth black cheek. "Why it's just like mine!"

My father bought me a small red glass engine, filled with yellow and red candies.

We got off the train and walked to Baker's. I had never been there, but my brothers had told me how much fun it was. They owned a grocery store and I want to go there and help my dad pick up stuff.

Mr. Baker had crates of vegetables sitting around the counter ready to sell, and six dozen eggs were in a wicker basket; I ran back and forth in excitement and fell headlong into the egg basket. Every egg broken!

Every time I saw the Bakers after that, someone would say, "Remember when you broke the eggs, Billy!"

I didn't remember a thing!

A Memory

We are in a train station,
My father and I.
I'm wearing a warm red coat,
A bonnet with ribbons.
I am three years old.

There are crowds of people
Screaming and laughing.
A woman hits her little son,
A man yells at his girl.
I'm frightened!

Then my father leans down
Enfolds my small hand
In his.
I feel safe.

The great black engine
Roars into the station,
Screeches to a stop.
He lifts me into the train.

A tall black man
Is selling toys
From a brown case,
Strapped to his shoulder.

Father buys me a red glass engine,
Smooth and shiny,
Filled with candies,
Yellow, blue, and red.

A small incident,
Almost lost in time.
Why do I remember?
Why do I weep?

The Dahlias

I am four years old. I have been put to bed early. I wake up at what seems like the middle of the night and hear music. It is coming from downstairs and I know it is my mother playing the piano, slow, lovely music. I listen for a minute, then I am suddenly overwhelmed. I get out of bed and run, sobbing wildly, and throw myself into my mother's arms crying, "Don't die! Please, please don't ever die!"

My mother enfolds me in her arms. "Hush, Darling," she murmurs softly. "I'm just fine. I'm not going to die. I'm right here with you. I'm not going to die for a long, long time."

Now I'm all grown up and I've come home for a visit. I'm sitting in my old room upstairs. The room is beautiful and familiar. The pristine white curtains cover sparkling windows. The four-poster bed is covered with the hand-stitched quilt my mother made. It is the log cabin pattern in shades of blue and white. It matches the rag rug on the polished floor.

My mother works too hard, taking care of the house, my younger sister, and invalid parents. My father helps but he is away working much of the time.

I'm sitting at a desk writing a letter. It overlooks the back yard where Mother has a dahlia garden. Each fall when she takes up the bulbs, she divides them, and the next year the garden is ever so much bigger. She trades bulbs with friends and neighbors so she has a great variety.

As I look out the window I see my mother come out and walk among the flowers. Just as I turn to reading and music for solace, she turns to gardening. She likes to feel the rich soil in her hands and she loves the sunshine. She plants and harvests all kinds of vegetables, but she is proudest of her flowers.

My mother is wearing a blue house dress and a pink flowered apron tied around her ample waist. She has pulled her hair back hurriedly and put it in a bun. Now curly wisps of hair are falling down on her neck. I can see, even from my place at the window, she looks tired and older. She doesn't know I am looking at her. I suppose she wouldn't like it.

She walks slowly up and down the rows of dahlias. Some are as tall as she is with blossoms the size of dinner plates. Some are small, maybe twenty-four inches high with blossoms on several stems. They are all colors, one is bright orange and looks like Raggedy Ann. There is a deep crimson beauty that stands five feet tall. Another is like spilled sunshine. There's a delicate pink blossom that is heavenly! Some blossoms are like velvet, others shaggy. Dahlias have no flower scent, just the fresh fragrance of summer.

She walks around picking dead leaves off here and there and putting them in the deep pocket of her apron. She stakes up one drooping plant whose large creamy flower is too heavy for the stem. She stops beside one tall dahlia, buries her face in the pale pink blossom. She stands motionless for minutes.

And suddenly I am overcome with grief. I want to run wildly down, as I did when I was four and cry, "Don't die, please don't ever, ever die!"

I know I can't do that. She would be embarrassed. I think I can't trust myself to speak. But I must go down.

I walk beside her; she turns and says, "Aren't my dahlias beautiful this year!"

I smile and say, "Just beautiful, Mother, just beautiful!"

Mary Ada

Whenever I think of Mary Ada, it makes me smile.

She came each summer to be with us for two or three weeks. One August we decided to dry corn. I bought twelve dozen ears and Mary Ada, Bill, and my brother Charlie offered to husk it. We pulled the table out by the seawall, heaped up the corn, and they got busy.

As I prepared the corn for drying in the kitchen, I could hear them talking and laughing—old friends. Sometimes they paused in their work and just sat quietly together, the only sound the soft lapping of waves against the shore and the wild cry of gulls.

In my bathroom I have a stack of washcloths carefully knit out of pastel cotton yarn. At Christmas my tree is a wondrous sight with sparkling ornaments of tiny colorful beads. Over my dining room table is a white and lacy angel suspended from the ceiling by a silver thread. We have dresses, and skirts, and hand-knit sweaters, and beautiful baby clothes. All these things the work of Mary Ada.

Often my granddaughter Andrea came over with her four little ones and when we all ate at one big table, Mary Ada was happiest. She loved the children. After dinner Eileen washed dishes, Mary Ada and Charlie dried, and I put away. Bill sat by and laughed. It's amazing how easy it is to do dishes when you combine it with friends and laughter.

I'm sure she was fond of all of us, but she was most fond of Eileen. I think they were kindred spirits.

In the evening Charlie made patterns for us and Mary Ada and I cut quilt patches from bright cotton. On Sunday evening we listened to the Gaithers. Mary Ada and Bill sang right along with them—old familiar hymns. She had a lovely soprano voice. They laughed at my range of six notes. And Charlie wouldn't even attempt it.

We didn't go out to fabulous restaurants, just to a funny little old place for Lake Erie perch. We didn't go on exotic trips. A trip to an Ohio farm market delighted her.

We just did ordinary things. Mary Ada made it special. We cherish the memories.

The Sunday Feeling

Is your church a joyous, exciting place to your children? A place that is familiar to them in every nook and corner; where they know the smell and feel and personality of each room as if it were their own? When I was little, mine was all of that. I knew it in all its moods.

It makes no difference where I am, in what faraway place, among strangers, among friends, or alone, if on Sunday morning I hear church bells ringing I am back once more in that little town in Ohio where I lived as a child. And my father is hustling us along to Sunday School to get there before the last bell rings. I can see the three little boys slicked down unnaturally and painstakingly and beautifully and the three little girls beribboned and starched. I can even yet feel my stiff petticoat against my bare legs and see my beautiful patent leather shoes. And I put my hand unconsciously to my hair to see if my bow is straight. I can see the quiet street, the familiar houses, feel the rest from workaday things, the awareness and goodness that was Sunday.

The church itself was warm and welcoming. Everyone was glad to see everyone else. It was a subdued joyousness, a quiet happiness invading all who entered. No one was self-conscious, no one was shy. We knew exactly what to do. We had been doing it for as long as we could remember.

I hurried to the Little Room. It was really the primary department which included everyone under school age. How we loved it! Mrs. Chamberlain was always there. No one else was ever in the Little Room when I was a child. She was wonderful. I thought she was the best singer in the whole world and she loved all of us, I am sure. I haven't sung so much or so well since I left the Little Room. We always sang *Precious Jewels*. And for some strange little girl reason, I always pictured the precious Jew---wells as a team of white horses, and the more loudly we sang the faster the horses galloped and I could see the manes and tails flying as Mrs. Chamberlain waved to us on to victory. I remember how surprised I was later, to find out the song about horses was merely about jewels.

And associated, too, with the Little Room was my idea that God wore a tweed peaked cap. I knew God was everywhere, God was love, and so forth. I could answer all the questions in chorus with the other youngsters but still He always wore a tweed peaked cap. And it was green tweed.

Sometimes we stayed for church. Sometimes we went to Grandpa's until our parents picked us up. Grandpa always sat in a wheelchair on the porch in nice weather or just inside the window if it was cold. He was bewhiskered and old and looked exactly like Santa Claus. To spend an hour with him was a joy. But whatever we did that glorious feeling of Sunday stayed with us all through the day.

And that was the Sunday mood.

How different was my church when empty. Once when I was sent on an errand to the church kitchen, I went upstairs and in the half darkness tiptoed in and sat in the church. It was cold and frightening. It had a different smell, it was utterly devoid of personality and it was most disappointing. And then I discovered the stained-glass window. I sat for a long time by myself. And I thought that if there was no music, no sermon, no warmth or friendliness, it was still enough—just to gather inspiration from the beauty of a window.

And that was another mood.

But the high point of the whole year, the very peak of the mountain, was the church supper. How different the church was then. How exciting to open the door and hear loud talking and laughing in the church! And women in aprons, flushed and triumphant from the kitchen. And the whole place simply permeated with the smell of good food, and over it all the rich wonderful aroma of coffee. Even the minister laughed out loud and we weren't afraid of him. And Mrs. Keyes, who on Sunday was a little bit uppity and reserved as befitted anyone who was "rich," smiled at the children and talked and wore an apron. We darted in and out and enjoyed ourselves hugely.

On church supper night we always put our coats in the Little Room on the chairs. Everyone did. There weren't any hangers, you just piled them up five and six deep, and everyone laughed and had a great time untangling them afterwards. Sometimes when the program after supper became a little dull, we younger girls sneaked down to the Little Room and tried on coats. Many are the times I have had on Mrs. Keyes' fur coat and Mrs. Logan's extra fancy hat. They always smelled exotically of perfume and kid gloves, and I still associate that with being "rich."

The suppers themselves were unsurpassed. The mashed potatoes melted in your mouth, the roast beef was cut off in huge luscious slices, the coleslaw was excitingly different. The fruit pies, flaky, golden, oozed berry juice. The ladies always asked you if you wanted seconds and before you could politely, but reluctantly answer, "No thank you," they heaped your plate again. Ah! I hope it hasn't changed.

After we finished eating, we all sang several hymns of the more peppy variety before we went upstairs for the program. And once, after the singing, they gave a prize, a family Bible, to the largest family. We all had to stand up and be counted and our family won. It embarrassed my two older sisters. They said big families were old-fashioned. But I loved it. I didn't care if we did all have big eyes and straight hair and look exactly alike, and I didn't mind standing up while they clapped. We *were* the biggest family and my mother and father were wonderful and I loved being part of it.

And that was the mood of fun.

But in all its moods the church was as familiar as home, as loved as Grandma's, as important as food; a cherished and beautiful memory of the goodness of childhood.

My Church

In a far-away place
Bells stir a memory
Back to a magic I once knew.
　Three little boys
　Slicked down unnaturally
　Three little girls beribboned and
starched,
　I can feel my stiff petticoat
　Against bare legs,
　Admire my patent-leather
shoes.
　I touch my hair.
　Is my bow on straight?
　Mother, miraculously serene,
　Father urging us to hurry,
　Last bell is ringing.
I am aware of quiet streets
Scent of roses,
And bells,
　I hurry to the Little Room.
　We sing *Precious Jew-els*,
　Exuberantly,
　Wondering what it means
　But not caring

As Mrs. Chamberlin
  Waves us on to victory.
  We stay for church
   Amid protests.
   It's long and boring
   When you're six,
   Until I discover
   The stained glass window.
If there was no music,
No sermon,
No flowers,
It would be enough,
Just to gather inspiration
From the beauty of a window,
   How different the church supper!
   Even the minister laughs out loud.
   Mrs. Keyes, who always smelled
of perfume
   And kid gloves
   Is wearing an apron.
   The aroma of unfamiliar food
   Fills the church.
   A prize to the biggest family!
   We stand up to be counted.
   How my sisters hated it!
   "How embarrassing!" they said.
   I didn't care if we did
   All have big eyes and look alike.
   I loved it!
Echo of bells,
Scent of roses,
Old memories.

Fifty Year Member Memory

About fifty years ago my husband Bill and I decided to build a log cabin. We had the logs delivered and stacked in the lot next door. We went to Sears and bought two shovels, two hammers, and one saw, and we started to dig the footer. The people on our road were skeptical. That's putting it mildly! They just shook their heads and looked skyward.

But as the weeks went by and it began to take shape, they came to look us over. They came out of curiosity because it was the first log cabin in that area. Also because an inexperienced young couple were attempting the impossible.

Many weeks later we had trouble with the heavy front door—four inches of thick heavy logs. We hung that door five times and it still wouldn't open or close. So we just nailed it shut! It was like your checkbook won't balance and you give it up and put it away. You think when you come back to it later, it will balance without any trouble. If you ever build a house, for Heaven's sake, get someone who knows how to hang a door. Don't do it yourself. We left the picture window out so that we could come and go. Lots of people climbed in through the window to see how we were getting along. I didn't know them, but they were friendly. We just kept right on working. You can't chat and build a house.

One day I am sitting on top of a ladder painting the ceiling. Ceilings are hard! I am wearing a pair of beat up shorts and an old shirt of Bill's. I am splattered with pain. Creamy white paint, in my hair, on my face, on my clothes. Ceilings are hard! Someone climbs in through the window and starts looking around.

"I have an extra brush," I say, hoping to get a little help.

"I'm afraid I'm no good at painting," he says. He looks around at all the work yet to be done.

"Can you hang doors?" I ask.

"No, I can't do that either," he says.

"What good are you?" I ask. I'm not mad, you understand. I'm just making conversation. After all I wouldn't expect any Tom, Dick, or Harry to come in off the street and be able to hang a door.

I go right on painting and splattering. Ceilings are hard!

Then he says, "My name is Bob Harriman. I'm the Pastor of the Presbyterian Church in Huron."

Well, you've never seen anyone scramble off a ladder that fast in all your life!

I splutter an apology. I can't shake hands, I am too grubby.

"I just came to invite you and your family to our services," he says.

And he climbs out the window and is gone.

A couple of weeks later we get ourselves all spiffed up and go to church. Bill carries Michael. Five-year-old Marty is with me. After the service, we go through the line.

The Rev. Harriman looks at me, and with laughter in his voice, says, "You clean up real good!"

This has been my church ever since.

Two Poems

Close, cloud-filled skies
Enfold me in comfort.

Ocean waves pound the shore.
I am so small.

In the quiet night
We share tears.

From the sea wall
The brilliant sky unravels,
Dissolves into night.

Sudden flash of blue
Glimpsed briefly on my plum tree,
Gone on wings of song.

My Christmas cactus,
Exquisite celebration!
Who tells you when to bloom?

Mrs. Ciderman's House

The house is small and old and weathered to a pale gray. The steps have deep grooves from the shuffle of many feet. When you open the green door, a little bell tinkles to tell the Cidermans they have a customer. The wide floor boards have been oiled to a deep brown. This is the place where we all flock to after school to spend a nickel if we are lucky enough to have one that day.

There are so many choices! Along the left side there's a long glass case displaying candy. Mrs. Ciderman, small and round, stands behind the counter cheerfully waiting while a child makes that momentous decision. You can get two mothballs, pure white and delicious with an almond in the middle. Or you can have two licorice sticks. They last a long time. There's a Clark Bar that you can eat off all the crumbly stuff and have a long strip of caramel to eat last. That was one of my favorites. Or a jawbreaker is lots of fun. They are two for a nickel so you can eat one now and take the other one home. They are so big you can hardly get one in your mouth at first. It changes color and flavor so you can take it out of your mouth every few minutes to see what color it is. Or you can ask a friend.

On another counter is a great round of yellow cheese. Mr. Ciderman stands here wearing a big white apron and carrying a wide knife. He will cut off a nice piece of cheese for you for a nickel. Behind the cheese there's a string of purple onions and a rope of pale garlic. Of course you wouldn't want to buy one of those, but I always liked the smell and the color. On the counter beyond the cheese are rows of little red, white, and blue paper bags with peanuts in the shell. They are nice, but are too much trouble.

In the far corner there's a huge barrel full of dill pickles. I loved the pungent smell of brine and dill. Tongs hang on the side of the barrel so you can fish out your pickle. A pickle is a good choice because you have a little left over when you get home.

Sometimes a small boy can't quite handle the tongs. He'll look surreptitiously around, then stick his hand in the barrel and grab a pickle. He wipes his hands on his pants and cheerfully munches on his green treasure.

All the smells and sounds and colors mingled together are pertinent to only one place—Ciderman's store.

Marjorie

On the north side of our town there is a small section of beautifully kept houses. The people who live here belong to the country club, send their children (never more than two) to exclusive summer camps, have daily help which they refer to as maids. They own at least two cars, the men work at high paying jobs and play golf, the wives wear designer clothes and play bridge. They call this place of theirs Magnolia Acres. The peasants on the south side of town refer to it as Whiskey Row.

In one of these houses is where Marjorie lives. She is nine years old. Her father is the manager of a large department store in the city. When Marjorie wants a new dress, her father brings ten dresses he thinks she might like. She models them for her parents. One year I got invited to watch. It's a big deal! She tries on one dress after another, comes slowly down the wide steps into the living room where her parents wait, actually taking notes! Marjorie may choose whichever ones she wants. Marjorie usually chose seven dresses.

Once she came to my house with her mother who was on some sort of committee with my mother. I was unhappy when I learned she was coming along. She wanted to swing on the rope swing under the maple tree. It had rained recently, and there was a puddle under the swing. She said she didn't care, she wanted to swing and I should push her. She was wearing a pink organdy dress with a wide sash tied in the back. The sash dragged in the mud and splashed onto her dress. Her mother said it didn't matter, she had plenty of dresses. My mother would have been very angry.

Now we are huddled together on the front porch of the Methodist Church waiting for Marjorie. Her church, the Presbyterian (my father says it is for rich Methodists), is across the street from ours. She will come with her parents. They will park on the lot beside the church and Marjorie will come around to the front door.

We wait breathlessly to see what she will be wearing this Christmas Day. We pretend it really doesn't concern us, and we pretend the cold doesn't bother us. But we wait.

"Here she comes," Rita says, "I see her father's car."

We squeeze together, the better to see.

Marjorie walks ahead of her parents. She is wearing a white fur coat, a white fur hat on her blond curls. She carries a white fur muff and is wearing high white boots.

"Fur coat! And she's only a kid!" exclaims Jane.

"Well, la de da!" Mary says.

"Who does she think she is?" from Patty.

"Queen of the May!" answers Buffy.

We make more smart remarks as Marjorie walks along, placing one foot precisely in front of the other, smiling at everyone, bobbing her little white fur hat, waving her little white fur muff.

"My father says her parents dote on her," Julia informs us.

"I wish I could be doted," I say.

"You couldn't be doted. You have six brothers and sisters."

So here we are, crowded together, never taking our eyes off Marjorie until she disappears inside the wide doors of her church.

In our dark wool coats, red mittens, stocking caps, and black boots, I think that down in our hearts, everyone of us envies Marjorie.

Waymans

Here in this apartment over Chapin's Dry Goods is where Mrs. Wayman and her two daughters live. The apartment has never been rented permanently before. It has five large rooms, dark and unattractive. Sometimes a salesman rented it for a few days while he worked in the vicinity, or a family might need it for a few weeks while major repairs were being done in their house. But no one had ever rented it for any length of time. Mrs. Wayman had signed a lease for a year!

Everyone concluded that, after all, she was a divorced woman with two daughters, Elizabeth, nine, and Dorothy, fifteen, and she probably had to make do with something inexpensive. All this we heard from Mr. Chapin himself, who had talked to Mrs. Wayman on the telephone.

We saw workmen coming and going for a few weeks. The day they were to arrive Claud Mooney, who drove the truck at my father's hardware store, offered to help the movers. My father told Mother it wasn't because he was so energetic, but rather because he was curious and wanted to be the first to see the Waymans, and anyway Claud Mooney had a brain like custard.

Claud Mooney helped all day and still hadn't seen anyone but the movers. But after the last trip up those steep stairs, he finally saw Mrs. Wayman.

"Are you the nice man who helped to move my things?" she asked.

"Yes Ma'm. I'm Claud Mooney."

"I just can't thank you enough," she paused. "May I call you Claud?"

From that moment on Claud Mooney was smitten.

You couldn't really blame him. A divorced woman with two children is not supposed to be beautiful, not in our town anyway. And she was very beautiful. She had soft dark hair in a funny pixie cut, golden skin, and you could drown yourself in her gray-green eyes. When she smiled, you simply melted and I guess that's what happened to Claud Mooney.

I heard Dad telling Mother that Mrs. Wayman had bedroom eyes. What are bedroom eyes anyway?

As more and more people went up to the apartment on one pretext or another, there were astonishing reports of beautiful furniture, polished floors, Persian rugs, and a small piano.

Then after one visit Claud Mooney reported that there was a picture of a naked man hanging on the wall! I didn't think that was such a big deal. I had three brothers and they all looked alike to me.

Elizabeth and I soon became best friends. She was welcome at my house anytime, but I wasn't supposed to go to her apartment. Whether it was because of the picture of the naked man, or because she was divorced, or became someone (Claud Mooney) had reported that a man had been seen going up to the apartment, my father laid down the law. Waymans was off limits!

So of course I had to see for myself. I always went there when I knew Dad was busy in the store, and I made sure that Claud Mooney was away on a delivery because he was a tattletale. I went there many times and Dad either didn't know it or chose to ignore it.

When I stepped into the Wayman's apartment the first time, everything was beautiful in that moment. It was a different world! The pale lemon walls, the polished floors, the lovely old rugs, the piano, the stacks of music, the books, the flowers! I was overwhelmed!

And on the wall a picture, almost life size, of a naked man. I stood and stared.

"Isn't it beautiful?" Mrs. Wayman said. "That's a picture of Michaelangelo's *David.* It's a very famous sculpture. Perhaps someday you will be able to see the real one in Florence, Italy. It's much more beautiful than the picture."

The kitchen was a real contrast. It was alive with color. Family pictures on the wall, fiesta dishes on the shelves, pots of flowers on window sills, a bright yellow cloth on the long table. It was a happy place!

"How about some fudge?" Elizabeth asked.

"I thought you'd think of that," her mother said.

She got a bright red stepstool, climbed up to the highest cupboard and brought down a plate of fudge. She cut off a big square for each of us. It was the most delicious fudge I had ever tasted. After that her mother always had fudge for us, just one piece from the highest cupboard.

The year I was twelve, our family went on a two-week vacation. When I got home, I could hardly wait to see Elizabeth. I had bought her a small gift and wanted to take it to her as soon as I got home.

The apartment was empty, not a sign of anything. I went to Chapin's Dry Goods store and asked Mr. Chapin what happened. He said they simply told him they were leaving, didn't tell him anything really, not why they decided to move or where they were going.

I never heard from Elizabeth again.

After that every time we made fudge we tried to make it like Mrs. Wayman's. She had given me the recipe and I followed it exactly, but it never turned out exactly the same. Perhaps it was because it didn't come from the happy kitchen or because I couldn't share it with Elizabeth.

Sometimes I wonder if their name was really Wayman. When I look back on it, I realize that Elizabeth never talked about her father or grandparents or friends. She never referred to a teacher or a school. Were they hiding from someone? Were they here in this small town under orders? Were they suddenly ordered to leave?

Once I asked Elizabeth where she used to live. She said the word Baden. Then she became terribly upset and started to cry. She made me promise that I would never mention that word, never tell anyone that she had said it. Of course I promised. Was Baden a place, a school, a person? I couldn't ask.

They never went out of town or had any company except once. One night my father worked very late at the hardware store. About two in the morning he closed the store and started to walk home. The bus from Pittsburgh had just arrived and Mrs. Wayman got off carrying a very heavy suitcase. Dad, who didn't believe it was safe for a woman to be alone on the street in the middle of the night, walked her to her apartment carrying her heavy suitcase. He didn't ask her where she had been and she didn't offer an explanation. Of course she may have made other trips out of town. Dad just happened to know about this one.

Later, Bill Harvey the policeman, teased Mother about seeing her husband on the street in the middle of the night with a beautiful divorced woman. Mother just laughed. She knew it already.

Sometimes in a far-off city, in some forgotten place, far from the small town where I knew her, I'll think I see her face in a crowd. Or I'll hear a laugh, or see a smile on someone's face, and just in that moment I'm reminded of Elizabeth. Did she grow up? Did she get married? Did she become a mother? And I'm filled with sadness.

Then I think about the fun we had riding our bikes, roller skating, buying dill pickles to eat on our way home from school, sharing secrets about boys, all the things you do when you are nine, ten, or eleven. And I remember the magic of the place where she lived. Then I smile and I'm glad for the few years I shared with Elizabeth.

Harvey Clarkson, Jr.

Harvey Clarkson, Jr. owns this store on the corner of Main and Pine Streets. It is the oldest store in our town. New and Used Furniture, Harvey Clarkson, Jr-Owner. Mostly used, I think. The locals call him Junior, but not to his face. He is small, and the way he scurries around the store nodding his head and waving his arms reminds me of the bantam rooster on Grandfather's farm. He has black hair, which he grows quite long and combs it sideways to cover the bald spot. I think it is kinda dumb because he isn't really hiding anything. He always wears a dark suit, white shirt, and blue bow tie.

Junior lives in an apartment over the store. He has lived there his whole life as his parents did before him. He has three rooms which he says is all anyone could possibly want. He cooks all his meals for himself, except for breakfast. Sometimes the store smells like boiled cabbage or bacon or chocolate cake. Then Junior sprays the store and the mixture of food and essence of lilac is unusual but not unpleasant.

Once a long time ago he got engaged to Elsie Ellenberger. She had great plans for a house with all new furniture. After all, the furniture was there in the store. But when Junior told her they were going to live over the store with the same furniture his parents had, she broke the engagement. Junior didn't care too much; he said he couldn't see how anyone could want anything nicer than his apartment over the store.

Much later Elsie married Cecil Cunningham who owned the Ice Cream Parlor. Mother said Elsie was getting old and had to settle, but I think she made a better choice. Now she can go downstairs and have a banana split or a hot fudge sundae. What could you do in a furniture store except go down and sit on a new chair? That could get boring after a few years.

Mother says Junior is set in his ways. I guess that means that his life is not very exciting. Every morning at exactly 7:30 he leaves his apartment by way of his outside stairs, crosses the street, and enters the restaurant. Home Cooking by Charles Cooper, known by the locals as the Chicken Coop. It's a lie about the home cooking because I've seen Carrie cooking right there in the kitchen of the restaurant. I suppose you couldn't say restaurant cooking, could you? Anyway it is the only restaurant in town so everyone goes there. Junior orders the same thing every morning. Gladys, the waitress, greets him cheerfully with, "What will it be, Mr. Clarkson?" She doesn't dare call him Junior to his face. She knows exactly what he'll order but he likes to study the menu and keep her waiting while he decides.

"Two eggs over easy, two slices of whole wheat toast, not too brown, four slices of bacon, crisp please, a jar of apple butter, coffee with real cream." When he drinks the last drop of coffee he calls Gladys. She is ready. She knows what comes next.

"Any fresh doughnuts?" He knows there are. There have been doughnuts every morning for ten years. "Two, please and more coffee. Be sure it's hot." Gladys is already on her way. Then at exactly 8:00 he pushes back from the table, leaves a quarter for Gladys, pays his bill, and crosses the street to open the store.

Sometimes on our way home from school Millie and I stop in the store to talk to Junior. He always pretends we are there to buy furniture. He shows us around and tells us about any new pieces he has or any old pieces that are antiques and probably very valuable. We bounce up and down on the chairs, he bounces too. He seems like one of us. We think he is very funny, but we aren't making fun of him. We like him.

Junior is always talking about traveling, but actually has never been any place except the store and the Chicken Coop. He told us he had an adventurous spirit but had never had time to travel what with the store and all. But some day he'd like to take a day off and go some place exciting.

Our small town is divided right down the middle by the railroad tracks. As far as I can tell, one side is just like the other. But the people on the north side think they are the aristocracy because Kitty Lou Rothwell lives over there, and she claims she is the direct descendent of Benjamin Franklin. So that makes the whole area think they are a cut above the south side. We ride over there on our bikes and to tell you the truth, it is just like our side.

Junior has never been across the tracks. He told us that some day he is just going to close the store and take the trip over there and see what it's like. He'll walk, of course; he has never owned a car, never learned to drive. He never needed one. After all he says he has everything anyone could possibly want right here.

So one day there is a sign on the door of New and Used Furniture, Harvey Clarkson, Jr. Gone on vacation. Back tomorrow.

He left early in the morning, packed a sandwich, a thermos of coffee. He is wearing a red bow tie which he feels is more appropriate for a vacation. He spends the entire day walking the streets, all five of them, on the north side. Finds a place under a big old oak tree on a children's playground, where he eats his lunch, drinks his coffee, and contemplates the joys of traveling.

He returns that evening in time to eat dinner at the Chicken Coop. He didn't cook his own evening meal as he always did. After all, he is on vacation. He orders the special, which is pot roast, fruit salad, apple pie, and ice cream. He leaves fifty cents for Gladys.

Then back to his apartment over the store, his adventurous spirit satisfied. Back to his own small comfortable world, a happy man.

The Potter

He is known in Amherst, Ohio, as Red the Potter.

Donald E. Redman lives in a hundred year old brown house on Spring Street. It has a large glassed-in front porch with wide shelves beneath the windows that are always filled with pottery: vases, bowls, casseroles, coffee mugs, and lamps. Anyone can stop in, look at the new pieces, buy anything they like, and enjoy a cup of coffee with Red and his wife Fritz.

It is difficult to describe Redman. He is an enigma. He is well-muscled, broad shouldered, athletic. He has a full growth of beard and mustache. He wears leather coats, heavy hand knit sweaters, earth type shoes, and a wide-brimmed leather hat. He often wears a very expensive wide turquoise bracelet that he bought in the southwest. Around his neck he wears a two inch shark's tooth on a silver chain.

Redman is an avid reader of good books, a connoisseur of the Civil War. He plays the piano quite well; his strong hands that shape bowls can play Mozart with a light touch. He has a beautiful flower garden, which he takes care of himself and gives arrangements to special friends. He loves animals, especially his seventeen year old cocker spaniel, Samantha. In some ways he is a loner, but he is a very loyal friend.

Redman wasn't always a potter. He graduated from Kent in 1953, taught school for eight years in Sandusky.

He returned to Kent for a Master's Degree in administration. As principal in Penfield, Ohio, he and the superintendent took an instant dislike to each other. When the super told him he didn't even like his smile, Redman decided he'd be happier teaching children. He returned to his home town and taught fifth grade until he retired in 1984. He had the reputation for being quite original and unorthodox in his teaching. He played soft classical music while students worked on projects. Once a year each student dressed as a character in his favorite book and performed for parents and friends. On that day there was standing room only.

In the summer of 1952 having always wanted to travel, he got a job on the lake boat, the William G. Clyde, carrying iron ore from Lorain to Three Harbors, Minnesota, or Duluth, back to Chicago, Conneaut, Erie, and Lorain. The salary was good. The work, sitting in the hold feeding the boiler, was back-breaking and dirty. The members of the crew were young and footloose. They were uneducated, heavy drinkers, prone to the use of off-color language, from entirely different backgrounds. In spite of that he found their stories fascinating.

In 1949 Redman was spending many hours in the Amherst library. He soon realized he was becoming more interested in the very attractive librarian, Eleanor Albright, than he was in the books.

Eleanor, known as Fritz, was an only child. She had never dated very much, never for any length of time. She attended Baldwin-Wallace College, but decided college was not for her. She was happy living at home, working in the library. Then she met Redman.

"What did you think when you met him?" I asked.

"I fell in love at first sight," she said. "He was different from anyone I've ever known. We could talk endlessly about everything. I was never happier than when I was with Red. When he asked me to marry him in 1953, it only took me a minute to say 'yes.'"

They moved to Sandusky and a year later their son Mark was born. Mark and his wife Becky and their three children now live in Indiana.

In the summer of 1989 Redman heard about a ride for the National Lung Association. He had always enjoyed riding a bike so he decided to try it. The ride started in Seattle and ended in Atlantic City. From the Pacific to the Atlantic on a bicycle!

If a rider earned $ 10,000 in pledges he got free airfare to Seattle. Out of three hundred riders, only ten got airfare. Redman was one of them. He rode an eighteen-speed Trek bicycle. They averaged sixty-five to seventy miles a day. Their nights were pre-planned. They stayed at campsites or colleges.

"What about food?"

"The food was wonderful all the way. It was prepared in advance by restaurants or churches," he said.

During the trip Redman celebrated his sixty-first birthday.

I asked him why he took the trip.

"I simply liked to ride a bike," he said.

"Was it fun?"

"I can't say it was fun as in fun and games," he said. "Rather it was the enjoyment of accomplishing a difficult goal, and inner rewards of success."

He was personally challenged to do something out of the ordinary, a pioneer spirit of relying on his own resources, and to a degree, tackling the unforeseen and to see if he could triumph and overcome the obstacles he might face.

In 1970 Redman attended a pottery class in Avon Lake. He was introduced to the pottery wheel and was instantly hooked.

"I've got to have my own wheel!" he told Fritz.

His first wheel weighed one hundred and fifty pounds. He set it up in the basement of their house. It was foot pedaled. Later he bought a smaller wheel, motor driven, controlled by foot. His kiln was electric.

"How difficult is it?"

"The first pot I made, just trying to make something symmetrical, I started at 7:00 and was still working on it 11:00! If you don't have a lot of patience, don't try it."

"The first thing I sold was a hand-formed bear. I sold it in Vermilion for thirty dollars. My first show was Vermilion Day in the park."

Redman knew he needed his own shop. Carrying supplies and finished pieces up and down from the basement was too difficult.

"I need a shop attached to the garage," he told Fritz.

Fritz had inherited $ 5000 from her father. She had been very close to him and had been saving the money for something special. She offered it to Red for his shop.

"Are you sure, Fritz?"

"I'm sure! I'd rather you were doing what you want instead of sitting home like a couch potato."

So with the help of his father, he built the shop.

His pottery is distinctive; no two pieces are alike, all hand done on the wheel, some hand-formed of animals. He shops for unusual colors, earth tones in green and brown, and soft blues. He has exhibited his pottery at Pioneer Days in Mill Hollow, the Vermilion art show,

Birmingham, and shops in Vermilion, Youngstown, and Sandusky. He has had private shows in Amherst, Huron, and Sandusky.

Redman is known for his teaching and for his pioneer spirit. The tangible signs of his creativity is in his pottery, always signed *RED*.

Hal and Joan

The scuttlebutt on the street was that a shrink and his artist wife had purchased the beautiful house on the lake. We just rolled our eyes and waited.

For the next week I watched a well-dressed, handsome man coming and going and assumed it was Dr. Rothumel. Then one evening he appeared at my door.

"Oh, Dr. Rothumel," I said.

"Just call me Hal, and this is Joan."

That was the beginning of a very special time for Bill and me.

Joan and Eileen and I spent many afternoons on the beach soaking up sun, breathing in the scents of summer, and laughing. Joan always brought her alarm clock; she would stay only a few minutes. When it rang, it was easy enough to shut it off and stay another half hour or so.

We made pickles at her house from an explosive crop of zucchinis. For a whole day I canned peaches with Hal's father. (I think he liked me!)

I got rid of the spiders in their shed because Joan is afraid of spiders. (Wimp!)

Grandson Matt pulled his little boat up on the rocks in front of the house. The lake kicked up quite suddenly, and the boat went out to sea. Just then Hal came home from the office. In his fine suit and expensive shoes, he jumped in the water and rescued the boat. Joan stood on the bank scolding and laughing.

Many Saturday nights we ate spaghetti at Cedar Villa. Fun, fun, fun!

The winter of the terrible blizzard Hal, in a big coat, boots, and a stocking cap, went up and down the street making sure everyone had food, medicine, and firewood. Joan made soup on some kind of little stove she had. Nothing ever tasted so good!

We had several vacations at Joan's wonderful farm in the mountains of New Hampshire. We explored the surrounding countryside, watched the fox in the meadow from the big window. Hal hooked up the tractor to the wagon and pulled us through the woods, over rough ground, in and out of ditches. Bill and I hung on for dear life while Joan screamed at Hal to slow down.

I guess the word that comes to mind when I think of those years is laughter.

Haiku

On an ancient tree
I count five crimson apples.
Let's make a pie.

From the topmost branch
The proud eagle stands alone
Envies the sparrow.

The Story About Bruce

Bruce is a lively little canary who lives with Michael and Lorraine. His two-tiered cage sits in the Music Room amid bright crotons, leafy ferns, sweet smelling miniature roses, and a fascinating fountain that endlessly pours water into space. Through the skylight he can see the leaves of the gum tree and the blue Carolina sky.

Bruce is a happy, bright yellow bird. He doesn't sing although Freddie at the Pet Shop assured Michael that Bruce was a male. The females don't sing, just twitter and flap their wings in a wimpy kind of way. They are hopeful that Bruce will sing eventually. He is an important member of the family. Mike and Lorraine never enter or leave the music room without a few words with Bruce.

Bruce loves music. When Michael plays Bach or Beethoven or Brahms on the piano, Bruce struts back and forth in his cage and chatters. But he does seem to prefer Bach. When Lorraine plays her violin, he sits motionless and watches with dreamy eyes. When she switches to fiddling, he jumps about in the cage in a canary version of *Turkey in the Straw*.

When they plan to go on a vacation, to be gone for several weeks, they are indecisive about what to do with Bruce. To find a reliable canary sitter would be next to impossible. They hesitate to take him along what with different climates and strange people. After a great deal of deliberation they decide to take him to the Horse Barn. Nathaniel, the owner of the farm, is a most reliable person and a good friend, and where Michael and Lorraine keep Thistle and Cactus, their palomino horses.

Bruce is no stranger to the animals at the farm since Michael has taken him there to introduce him when they first got him. Bruce already knows Thistle and Cactus, Webster the brown collie, and Annabel the black cat. They felt that Bruce would be comfortable and happy there for a couple of weeks.

Two weeks later they return to the Horse Barn to pick up Bruce. In the car Lorraine says, "Michael, the band on Bruce's leg is loose. Do you think he lost weight?"

"It seems unlikely," Mike says, "Anyway it would hardly be noticeable on his small leg."

"Besides," Lorraine says, "The expression on his face is different. He looks confused, like he doesn't know me!"

"Perhaps he's aggravated because we left him so long. I'm sure Nathaniel was good to him. There's no reason for Bruce to be traumatized over anything at the Barn. Let's not worry about it Lorraine. He'll be relaxed and happy after a few days back home."

Days went by; Lorraine was exceptionally attentive to Bruce. She talked to him, played her violin, and fiddled. Bruce continued to look depressed.

"I don't think it's Bruce," she told Michael.

"What do you mean, it's not Bruce? Of course it's Bruce!"

"I think something happened to Bruce and Nathaniel replaced him with another look alike canary. Come over here and look."

"Why don't we just ask Nathaniel?" Mike said.

"We couldn't do that. He's our friend. We'd hurt his feelings if nothing happened. And you know he hasn't much money, if he spent $ 125.00 for a new canary, it's because he likes us and doesn't want us to be unhappy."

Lorraine leans in closer to the cage. "Wasn't Bruce a brighter yellow?"

"He does look a little pale," Mike said.

"Maybe he had a nervous breakdown at the Barn—all those animals around!"

"Perhaps it's just the way with canaries," Mike said, "they get paler as they get older, just like people."

"I'm sure you're right, Michael." She talks to the canary. "You're home now Bruce, we won't leave you again!"

"Quit worrying Lorraine! Of course it's Bruce."

Things settled down. They talked things over with Bruce as they always had. Mike played the piano, introduced new music, Lorraine played her violin and fiddled. If Bruce seemed less than pleased, they attributed it to maturity. Bruce was no longer a teenager. They put it out of their minds. It was a relief to quit worrying about it.

A few months later Carol and Richard came for the weekend. Richard has always been fond of Bruce. He stood by his cage to talk to him.

"I never knew Bruce had that dark brown spot under his chin," Richard said.

"He doesn't have a chin," Mike said.

"Who doesn't have a chin? I hate men without chins, shows lack of courage!" Carol says, as she comes from the kitchen.

"We're talking about Bruce!"

"Bruce the canary?"

"That's the one."

"Canaries don't have chins."

"Then how can he have a spot under it?"

"Who's chin are we talking about?" Lorraine is just entering the room.

"Bruce's!"

"Bruce the canary?"

"The same."

"Canaries don't have chins," Carol says as she leaves to inspect the cooking.

"Then how can he have a spot under it?"

"Who's chin are we talking about now?" Lorraine asks.

"Bruce's!"

"Bruce the canary?"

"The same!"

"Well, there's a spot there that wasn't there before," Richard says. "Are you sure this is Bruce? Doesn't look like Bruce. Legs are too skinny."

"Who has skinny legs?" Carol calls out from the kitchen.

"Bruce!"

"Bruce the canary?"

"Don't start that again!"

Now the old suspicions return. One day Bruce begins to tear out pieces of the paper on the bottom of his cage. Apparently he is making a nest. He makes it all soft and cozy in the upper level of his cage. He sits there day after day looking sad and miserable.

Now they are convinced it isn't Bruce. They change his name to Lucy. They bring her little treats: spinach, broccoli, red grapes, and millet. She doesn't lay an egg; she doesn't sing. She doesn't even twitter, just sits and looks unhappy.

"She's lonely, that's what is wrong with her," Michael says.

They go back to the Pet Shop and buy a bright new canary. Freddie, the Pet Shop person, assures them that this one is a male and will probably sing. No, he can't guarantee it will sing; he's pretty sure.

They name him Granville. They put him in the cage and introduce him to Lucy.

She stays upstairs on her nest; Granville stays silently downstairs.

Then suddenly on the fifth day, Granville breaks the silence with a song, a song so joyful, so passionate, that his whole small body quivers. If you listen carefully, you can discern two different songs. A dozen times a day now he sings. He stands outside Lucy's nest and sings his little heart out.

But Lucy doesn't lay an egg. Someone told Lorraine that farmers use to put a fake egg under a hen to encourage her to lay. Lorraine found a very small white bead and put it under Lucy. Lucy didn't seem to object but looked at Lorraine as if this was some sort of game. After a few days, she flipped it out of her nest.

For six months Lucy sat on the nest, never laid an egg, looked frustrated and sad. For six months Granville sang his beautiful songs.

Now they decided to buy a mate for Lucy. But Freddie, the Pet Shop person, persuaded them to buy a pair since Lucy was, at most, an enigma.

They named the pair Lorrie and Popogeno. Lorrie laid four eggs. Three of them hatched. They named the three Snap, Crackle, and Pop. Lucy was appalled! A couple of musicians to name their canaries after cereal!

Lucy was sure Lorraine and Michael were losing it.

Now Lucy became more and more despondent. She began to pull her feathers out, wouldn't eat. Michael and Lorraine thought she was jealous of all the new birds. Her home had been disrupted. Granville sang, not only to her, but to all the canaries. All that twittering and chirping was just too much.

Lorraine decided to give Lucy to the Cleaning Lady. She had always liked Bruce, then Lucy. Perhaps she could make her happy and energetic again.

So now Lucy is living in the bright yellow kitchen with the Cleaning Lady. Her small cage hangs in the window overlooking the vegetable garden. There's music from the radio, granted it's not Bach, but it's cheerful. There's always the smell of coffee and bacon and, sometimes, cookies. The Cleaning Lady talks over her troubles, which are many, with Lucy. Lucy is important. She seldom thinks about Granville or the Music Room.

So here in the kitchen, rejuvenated and important, lives Lucy.

Or---is it Bruce?

George

There's this cat in our neighborhood. He's a pale yellow short-haired cat with amazing golden eyes. This cat has real class. He strolls up and down our street, eats wherever he find something that appeals to him. Some days he eats with Velvet and Lace, two old spinster cats who live with the Figgins. They are all atwitter when young yellow cat comes for lunch. They purr like a couple of teenagers.

Perhaps he goes to Kim's or Sandy's or Nita's or across the street to Jane's for dessert. Or he may start at Jane's and go the other way.

One day when a few neighbors were together and yellow cat joined us, someone said, "What's this cat's name? Does anyone know?"

And I said, without thinking, "It's George."

"How do you know? Is it your cat?"

"No, it's not my cat. He just looks like a George, kinda devil-may-care, a macho cat."

So, George it is.

George attends all picnics, barbecues, bonfires, and potlucks. He likes hot dogs, hamburgers, and ribs, but actually prefers steak, medium rare. He'll eat most vegetables, but sniffs at parsnips. Chocolate cake has him doing catwheels.

One day Nancy, the attorney on our street, noticed that George had an infection in his eye. She took him to the veterinarian and had his eye taken care of plus all his shots, and other things George would soon as leave forget. But actually he was never interested in having a family, getting up at night and all that stuff.

Nancy doesn't want to keep George in her house because her black and white cat Lentil (known to the neighbors as Killer) doesn't get along with George.

Nancy calls Jane to see if she'll take George. Jane worries about George; Jane worries about all cats everywhere. But she already has a cat named Max (Sendak's Max). Max is a real wimp, runs and hides under the bed if Jane so much as drops a marshmallow.

Andrea can't take George. She already has Velvet and Lace, Beau and Maggie, two hugs labs, Teddy the hamster, and four kids. George would be one too many!

George is back on the street.

Nita isn't well; she lives alone and depends on the neighbors for help and companionship, and very often, food. After all it isn't much trouble to put in an extra potato or bake a small pie. Nita knows all our business. No one cares. We all like her. She's a character.

George knows Nita is lonely and he seldom misses a few minutes with her although it's on his own terms. He doesn't like schedules. It ties him down.

This goes on for months. Now it's getting cold, and George is still on the street.

One day we learn that Nita has become much worse. She has been taken to the hospital, and later to a nursing home. As the days go by, we know that she can never return home.

Her house stands empty. Someone has a brilliant idea. Why not let George live in Nita's house! It's the perfect solution!

So here's George. His home is in a good location. It has a living room, kitchen, three bedrooms, two baths, a glassed-in front porch, a big yard, and just minutes from beautiful Lake Erie. Neighbors supply food and take care of the litter box.

If you've a mind to visit George, he's on Mansfield Avenue, just three houses down from Cleveland Road. It's that yellow house with white trim. You can't miss it.

George will probably be sitting in the picture window in an easy chair. Just sitting there, not reading, just cat watching. You can visit him anytime. It won't matter to him one way or the other.

The Midwest

I like the four seasons of the Midwest, each one different and full of surprises. I like the people. Midwesterners are, for the most part, intelligent, down-to-earth, hard-working, generous, caring, but not intrusive.

In summer there's Lake Erie teeming with wildlife, always fascinating. It's a time for swimming, fishing, and picnicking. We wear shorts and sandals and bask in the sunshine. In the evening we watch spectacular sunsets.

By the end of summer the whole world turns to glorious shades of red and gold. We take long rides and get lost on county roads and find small serene villages. We stop at a farmer's market where the abundance of fruits and vegetables is beautiful and amazing, none to equal it anywhere. We buy our favorite apples, Jonathans, Macs, Winesaps, and munch apples happily as we explore.

We have bonfires by the lake on nippy nights. Friends wander by to share a quiet time or a few laughs.

Then one day we wake up to a different world.

> *No cloud above, no earth below,*
> *A universe of sky and snow!*

My chimenea is a big old snowman, my picnic table is a cave. Every branch on every tree is dazzling in the winter sunshine. Out come the sleds, the skates, the skis. We wear bright sweaters, fuzzy warm coats, and funny stocking hats.

On cold wintry days we sit by the fire and welcome solitude. We read a good book and look out upon a white world. Then all too soon the holidays have come and gone.

And before you know it, the daffodils and crocuses are popping up and spring is in the air. It's time to think of beautifying the lawn, planning vacations, buying new clothes. We know we can't fit it all in. But it's springtime and we're starting all over again.

The Midwest has everything.

Project Dr. Suess

My third grade students combined reading, writing, English, and art into a project that snowballed into an exciting experience.

The project was Dr. Suess, the favorite author of the eight-year-old set. After reading about his "not-really any kind of animal" the children became so intrigued by the delightfully funny pictures, and clever lines, that they wanted to make a Dr. Suess figure of their own.

My own two children and I scoured the beaches of Lake Erie for just the right pieces of driftwood. Each child then chose one he liked and painted it with tempera paint, any color or combination of colors. To make their animals even more fantastic they brought in bits of fur, feathers, sequins, buttons, and beads for decoration.

Now they gave them names. Bertram with Buttons, Bump-bump McDuff, Sequin Sam, Jiminickle, Barrel Baby. One little girl simple named her animal George.

They were so attractive and unique that Jim Barton, the principal, took them to a principals' meeting where they were displayed for several weeks. Huron residents had the opportunity of seeing the animals on display in the Public Library during National Library Week.

We decided we should tell Dr. Suess about our wonderful animals. In English class the children wrote letters, the best one to be sent to the author-artist. The letters were all so good and so funny that finally they were all bundled up, along with a picture, and sent to Dr. Suess.

In less than two weeks, a letter was received from Mrs. Dr. Suess, telling us how much they had enjoyed the letters. She sent a picture of Dr. Suess working on a new book. She left a space at the bottom of the letter for Dr. Suess to say "Hello."

He signed, "Thanks from my dog and me." He drew a picture in colored pencil of the little dog he wrote about in so many of his stories.

As a perfect climax, one of the mothers, Myra Gallant, took the letter and picture and had copies made for each child in the class to keep as a treasured memento.

Last Day

The room is empty now.
All that remains
Is the smell of chalk and books.
On the floor are scraps of yellow paper,
A blue crayon,
A small worn sneaker.
Don't run in the halls!
Don't run in the halls!
Echo of laughter.

They learned to read,
To write and count.
To be aware of life beyond this place,
And countries far away,
To browse through maps
And plan adventure trips.
We polished rocks, fragments shaped
By rain and wind and water,
Discovered sunrise and evening sky
Secrets in stones!

On winter days we shared *Snowbound*,
In Spring
We talked of daffodils.
We painted murals
To the sweet sounds of Mozart and Brahms.
But what about the real world?

That, *fair*,
Is not a universal word,
That dreams seldom *do* come true.

Did I fail them?
These small eager children?
And yet—and yet
When someone later asks,
What did you do?
My heart sings!
I was a teacher.

Fragments, Too: Pieces of Wilma

The Recipe Box

My most treasured keepsake is the old wooden box full of time-worn recipes left to me by my mother. I live in the past as I browse through them.

Here's one for cookies. I can see my mother and Grandfather sitting at the kitchen table eating warm, soft ginger cookies and drinking coffee out of blue mugs.

Sunshine cake! Every Easter the table was aglow with daffodils!

This one makes me laugh. It is a recipe for spice cake. Beside it is a note. This cake is no good; don't make it. Why did she keep it? Why not just throw it out?

Here's her famous recipe for cloverleaf rolls. I laugh when I read, "two eggs if they're cheap." How my sisters and I have tried unsuccessfully to duplicate those rolls.

Elderberry pie every Sunday. (Where do you get elderberries now?) My mother said I always stood between her and the rolling pin when I was three. Then I would make little slightly used pies for my father.

I can shut my eyes and see and smell the chicken and dumplings on that happy day when my brothers came home from the war, safe and sound.

Here's her recipe for mustard pickles. Mother put them in a huge crock and covered it with grape leaves. No need to can them, they went too quickly. My glamorous cousin Anne used to come from Pittsburgh and headed straight for the mustard pickles.

Sometimes these recipes make me weep. I miss her so! But mostly I'm filled with laughter and feel blessed to have such warm memories. My mother didn't just cook food, she created happiness.

The New Car

In 1957 my husband was diagnosed as having Multiple Sclerosis. At the time I was earning the munificent sum of ninety dollars a month. I scrambled to earn a teaching degree, keep two children, and make dozens of trips to the hospital fifty miles away. We lived mostly on peanut butter sandwiches and carrot sticks. After a year Bill came home to rehabilitate. During that time he entered a contest sponsored by WTOL Toledo. He wrote a short poem about his favorite movie, *The High and the Mighty*. There was only one prize! What chance did we have? Then one wonderful day we got a phone call saying we had won a car. We were invited to Toledo to accept our car on television. We were taken to dinner first and treated most royally. Then to the television station to see our car. What a car it was! A '63 Corvair Monza, brilliant red exterior, all white leather interior. We couldn't believe our eyes! We loved that car! It came at the right time to give us a much-needed lift. We drove it for years. It was a beautiful and exciting car—our all-time favorite

*Palmolive Soap**

I like Palmolive Soap for dozens of reasons. In the first place my little sister Apples has for the first time in the history of the family washed off the high water mark and gone to regions beyond. It's a great thing, knowing she's white again.

Then there's Gramps. He insists on spilling soup on his whiskers on soup day. But does that get Mom down? I should say not! She runs for the Palmolive and his whiskers, once a tell-tale gray, take on that Santa Claus appearance and become soft and silky.

Take my love-sick brother Bobbie. He simply loves it. Since we've changed to Palmolive, I've known him to stay under the shower for as long as an hour and a half at one standing. He sings, he whistles, he lathers with rich creamy lather, rinses it off and begins again. The line forms to the left in the hall. We call it the Palmolive Brigade.

My brother Bill just got his sheepskin last week and is now on the trail of a job. He travels via thumb. Luggage must necessarily be light. He takes with him a gift of gab, a clean shirt, a toothbrush, and a cake of Palmolive soap. With that he expects to set the world on fire.

Mom uses it because…well, Pop is a traveling salesman and she realizes that other babes in other towns may have learned the secret of that schoolgirl complexion and she takes no chances. She needn't worry, she's lovely. Pop thinks so, too.

As for me, I'm trying to hook a man and between you and me I've almost got him hooked.

That leaves Pop and he agrees with the rest of us because Palmolive is so inexpensive and after all the family must eat.

Hold everything! I forgot Carlo Mae Agnes. Since we started using Palmolive on her, it has become most disconcerting. We never know where she is, when she enters a room, or when she is hiding under the table or in a bedroom. She has completely lost that doggie odor.

Like Living in Years Past

"Will you have your napkin tied around your neck in the colonial manner?"

I smilingly consented and our waiter deftly tied a thirty-six-inch square of snowy linen around my neck. We were dining (and I use the word deliberately) in the candle-lit garden of the King's Arms Tavern in Colonial Williamsburg.

The waiter wore a white ruffled shirt, powder blue knee breeches, white stockings, and black buckled shoes.

From the Bill of Fare I selected frosted fruit shrub, fine broiled fish from local waters, "sallad" of green stuff, Sally Lunn bread, sweets and pastries.

Wine was available as stated, "Drink no longer water, but use a little wine for the stomach's sake." 1 Tim. 5-23.

We sat on high backed benches at heavy wooden tables. The atmosphere was leisurely. The ancient mulberry tree in the corner of the garden may have been there when the young Colonel George Washington of Mount Vernon entertained friends in about 1772.

We had the feeling that we had stepped back across a bridge of years into the 18th Century when Williamsburg was at its glorious height, history was in the making, and entertainment was at its lavish best.

*Editor's note: *Palmolive Soap* was Wilma's first published submission and was awarded a $1000 prize in 1930.

When I was fifteen years old, I was studying violin with Professor Ostheimer. I had a lesson once a week, and on other days I went to the conservatory at the college and practiced in one of the practice rooms.

I liked going to the conservatory. It was in an old ivy-covered building on the campus. When I opened the heavy doors and went inside, I was immediately in a different world. I liked the smell of old wood, of polished floors, but most of all the sound of music permeating the whole building.

I stopped at the office to say hello to Mary, the professor's young wife. They had just recently been married. She was very proud of her professor husband and he adored her.

I went up the wide stairs to the second floor to the little room assigned to me. As I passed the practice rooms, I stopped to listen. One student was working on a Mozart concerto, another one was struggling with Bach. In another room two students were having a great deal of difficulty with a duet.

I thought Professor Ostheimer was very handsome for an older man. I suppose he was in his forties, but at fifteen anyone over thirty seemed old. He was German, talked with an accent and sometimes mixed up his metaphors, which made me laugh. His voice was gentle and encouraging. When he played the violin, I was transported to a world of either such joy or anguish to make one weep. And when he conducted the orchestra in his formal black and white, it was to fall in love.

He sometimes came up to the practice room to help me with a difficult piece. He always adjusted my violin under my chin and checked the small black velvet pad that protected my shoulder. Then one day, just for an instant, he very lightly and almost tenderly placed his hand on my small breast. I stood dumbly, unable to move. Then he was gone. I thought maybe it was accidental. After all, he had been adjusting my violin. I didn't know if it meant anything or not. It was only for a second. It wasn't anything, I assured myself.

Then it happened the next time, and the next time, never any different, just that light touch and he'd leave. I decided I wouldn't go to the practice room any more. I would miss the conservatory, but I had become uneasy and confused.

Later Professor Ostheimer asked me to play in the symphony orchestra. For the next three years I practiced with the orchestra once a week. He was always kind and considerate to me as he was to all of us.

A few years later his Mary left him. No one ever heard from her. I still don't understand it.

Harry is an optician. He sits in the optical department of a large store and grinds lenses. Sometimes the customers sit for hours, rubbing tired eyes, waiting for their glasses to be finished. It makes Harry nervous having someone breathing down his neck. Sometimes he breaks lenses and then all hell breaks loose in the department. Harry threatens to quit. But he is good at what he does and the boss calms him down and he stays.

Harry is strange. He has pale skin that breaks out in red splotches at times. His hair is long and lank and blond. He has long slender fingers that can handle the most delicate lenses. His clothes belong in a ragbag although they are always clean. He works six days a week in his little cubbyhole at the back of the store. He makes twenty dollars a week. He has a wife, Mildred, who is pregnant. Mildred is expecting twins. Harry is desperately trying to save enough money to pay for her hospital stay. He has no insurance, he doesn't own a car.

Harry saves money by doing without meals. He told me he eats soda crackers, lots of soda crackers, then drinks plenty of water. He then feels full and can skip several meals.

Harry suddenly gets a call from his neighbor. Mildred has gone into labor, three weeks early! Harry hasn't saved enough money. The boss lends Harry his car and I drive. We get Mildred and race to the hospital. They want money up front. They refuse to take Mildred. We go to a second hospital. Harry is frantic. They refuse to take Mildred. Mildred is now screaming and moaning in pain. Harry is trying to sooth Mildred who is now almost ready to deliver.

We rush all the way across the city to a third hospital. Harry is cursing the hospital, the nurses, the doctors, the whole world.

The third hospital takes Mildred. It is too late. One twin is dead. For a long time no one dared to speak to Harry about anything. What could you say after all?

The Bike Ride

By a circuitous route
I ride my bike
to the top of Hallowell Hill.

Look down at my town,
see my gray stone house,
the creek that runs around.

I start down.
Feel the pedals under my feet,
know each bump on the road.

Gather speed,
Now I'm flying!
Wheels barely touching the earth.

The wind ruffles my hair,
stings my eyes,
blurs the blues of summer.

I'm one with the wind,
the scents, the sounds,
and the secrets of the world around me.

The ghost of a little girl,
laughing at the pure joy
of simply riding a bicycle.

Come, get your bike.
We'll ride together.
You and I.

Huron Writers' Club

The Huron Writers' Club started away back in the sixties. Anyone was welcome who was interested in writing. At first we had only five or six, later it increased to twenty-two. We met at a member's house. Everyone had something to read. We usually had coffee and cookies. It seemed like people were more relaxed and friendly if they could chomp on a cookie.

Helen Ball, a petite, white-haired woman never missed a meeting. She always brought something she called popcorn, but she assured us it was better for you—no fat, no sugar, no calories, no taste. When you put it in your mouth, it immediately absorbed every bit of moisture, kinda like eating a cotton ball. But we just rolled our eyes and ate at least one of whatever it was. We all liked Helen.

She originally came from Huron. After her husband died, she moved to California where she later remarried. When he died, she moved back to her hometown. She said to us, "To tell you the truth, Girls (she always called us girls), I was glad when he died."

Helen wrote delightful stories about animals, usually chickens. I like chickens myself because I once knew a chicken named Doris that I was quite fond of. One story was about a big red rooster named Harry. He ruled the barnyard. A real dude of a chicken. He strutted around showing off to all those ditzy blond hens. The old dog Newton had just about enough of Harry. He attacked him from behind and pulled off his gorgeous tail feathers. Harry was devastated! No more was he King of the Barnyard. He was a pitiful sight! Sally, who owned him, had to do something. She got out her new feather duster and tied it securely to Harry's stub of a tail. Once again Harry was King of the Barnyard. I don't know if she ever sold any of these stories. I suppose chickens do not have the appeal of a Lassie.

Edna and Hazel, the fat retired teachers, met with us in the summer. They rented a cottage at Mitiwanga. We didn't actually call them fat, but each one weighed about two hundred pounds. They always talked about dieting but more as a joke. I think they were comfortable with themselves. They were both quite attractive but different. They wore bright flowered dresses and unusual jewelry. They were working on a novel, but in the six years we knew them, it never got finished. I think for them the meetings were a social thing and we were happy to have them. They were both funny and always had something to contribute.

I don't know if this story was original with them, but at least we hadn't heard it. Hazel decided to wash clothes. She gathered up all the dirty laundry into the big brown basket, took it to the basement and dumped the clothes into the washer, added detergent. She had been weeding flowers, collecting shells, and hunting colored glass on the beach. She looked down at her soiled white shirt, her dirty jeans. She looked around. No one here! What the hell! She stripped off all her clothes, put them in the washer; and naked as a jay bird, ran up the steps— only to meet the meter man on the landing.

He was momentarily paralyzed. He recovered because Edna said he read the meter the next month after announcing his arrival in a *very loud voice.*

When I asked Ruth Beiswinger to join our group, someone said to me, "You'll be sorry you ever asked her. She'll dominate everyone!" So it was with some trepidation that I looked to the next meeting. She turned out to be quite the opposite, pleasant and gracious.

As I learned more about her I could understand why a person might call her dominating. She had been a foster parent for twenty years. Over that time she had taken care of forty children, sometimes just one, sometimes three at a time. Some were newborn children, some teenagers. The length of time varied; it could be for a few days or a year. She kept the children warm, well fed, clothed, and safe. She didn't allow herself to become fond of them. She knew it would tear her apart when they left. Although she did adopt one little girl.

She read at almost every meeting, never about the children, but about her younger days when she lived in Boston. She had a few idiosyncrasies (but haven't we all?). She refused to have a television in her house. Her husband was crazy about television and would go to different stores to watch whatever was showing. Someone gave him a television, but Ruth got rid of it the next day.

When we went to her house for a meeting, we knew to put on our warm undies and take an extra sweater because her house was never warm.

Ruth seemed almost grateful that she'd been invited.

A young couple just out of college, and recently married, joined our group. She had a job as a secretary; he didn't have a job because he was going to be a writer. She said she would give him one year and then she was going to start a family. If he hadn't made it as a writer by that time, he promised her he'd get a job. They came to a few meetings after that. He was working on a novel.

Jane Linhart entered contests. That was way back when you could write something interesting or different in fifty words or less. She had won refrigerators, electric stoves, mattresses, kitchen ware, food, you name it. She was great fun, always tried out her entries on us.

Eileen Wikel wrote poetry. It always rhymed, but not the sing-song variety. She did it quite well with an ability to express emotion through delicate shadings and variations. She especially liked to write about cardinals. She wrote happy poems, sometimes funny poems. Her laugh was contagious. When Eileen laughed, everyone laughed.

Sometimes she'd call me on the phone in the middle of the day. "I'm writing this poem and it doesn't sound right. Do you have time to listen?"

"That last verse. Something doesn't sound just right. It doesn't read well. Read it again," I'd say.

"I'll work it over—call you back."

Later, "I think I've got it. Listen to this."

"Much better! Leave it alone now."

Eileen sold many of her poems, wrote her own Christmas cards, and contributed poetry to the church newsletter.

She wrote a column for the Hinckley newspaper for three years. She was quite knowledgeable about the people and history of Hinckley because her grandparents had lived there. She spent many vacations with them while growing up.

Ruth Brown sold every story she ever wrote about raising mink on their mink farm. They were all funny, although how you could see humor in those horrible, smelly mink I don't know. When she had her arms up to her elbows mixing mink food, while she was pregnant, she'd turn it into something hilarious.

Ruth could write anytime, any place. Some people have to put everything in order first and then sit down to write. Not Ruth! We'd all be writing or reading at her house, dishes stacked in the kitchen, an occasional mouse hunting food. It didn't bother Ruth one bit, not while she was writing.

She herself was always especially neat, well groomed, and pretty. She liked to wear long-sleeved white shirts and small bright ties. She was working on a novel, very original about a man who discovered oil in a cemetery, causing all sorts of problems. She never got it finished.

James, a minister, was writing a novel. He was very excited about joining our group. He and his wife owned one car, and after a few months it seemed that on meeting night the car was never available because his wife needed it. I offered to pick him up since I'd be going right past his house. On the next night when I beeped the horn for James, his wife came out and informed me that instead of wasting time writing a novel, they had decided he could spend more time with her.

Ethelberta lived on a farm in a wonderful old house. Her country kitchen was big enough to seat twenty-two at the antique table. If our meeting happened to be at her house in early June (and I'm sure we arranged it that way), she served strawberries from her berry patch and cream so thick you had to take it out of the bowl with a spoon, a real treat that.

She wrote a column called *The Farm Wife's Window* from 1940 to 1962. She had it syndicated and it was published in many small towns in Ohio. She wrote about her life as a farmer's wife, doing her duty and raising five children. Her columns were about ordinary things with a true knowledge and a dry sense of humor. She wrote about all the things she saw and experienced from her window at Meadow Brook Farm.

Margaret Nichols wrote stories about Indians. She had spent some time on an Indian Reservation and became interested in their culture. One story took place in ancient times. It was about a young couple who had just had a baby. They had heard many tales about Indians and their cruelty. And there stood an Indian chief knocking at the door. What to do? Get a gun? Barricade the door? He knocked again. Surely if he meant to harm them, he wouldn't knock. They opened the door cautiously. The tall silent Indian handed them a beautiful pair of moccasins for their baby boy. She sold this story.

Patty, middle-aged, well educated, interested in writing short stories, came to three meetings. She didn't read anything or make any comments during the first two. About halfway through the third meeting she stood up and said, "There isn't a single person here who knows anything about writing. All you do is eat! It's been a waste of my time!" With that she walked out the door.

Complete stunned silence for a minute. Then someone laughed, then we all laughed and someone said, "Pass the cookies!"

Bette Hinman was an enigma, very well educated, sophisticated, and quite beautiful. She came from New York City and how she ended up in the small village of Berlin Heights was a mystery. She never talked about her life in New York.

She had lived in Hollywood where she had an answering service for Raymond Burr. She couldn't say enough good about him, his kindness, his generosity, and his beautiful eyes. Through him she met many famous movie stars.

She wrote a column for the Elyria paper for several years. She found it quite boring, all about social affairs, but she needed the money.

She was fascinated by coincidences. She collected them for her stories. Everyone had something to share and one night our meeting lasted until eleven o'clock relating coincidences. (If not, what else?)

She also wrote about premonitions, why they happened to some people and never to others. She wanted to figure out what kind of person had an ability to anticipate an event. Were they different in other ways? Just as she herself was a mystery, so were her stories.

On a bright note, she belonged to the Trout Club and when it was her turn to have the writers, we all enjoyed a trout dinner before the meeting.

A Midwest Sense of Community

I compare my community to a tossed salad. Each ingredient tastes good and is good for you, but each one is entirely different. The link that holds our separate days together is the lake.

There are no gates to keep anyone out of my community, no hard and fast rules and regulations. You may paint your house the traditional white, or bright yellow if you choose. You may have one cat or four if you like cats all that much; really some do!

There is a diversity of people in my community. Each life has a story, each one unique!

One man goes wherever there is a high bridge to be built. Another one works for the airlines. There are teachers, a contractor, a lawyer, a truck driver, a librarian, a school bus driver, a doctor, a photographer, a massotherapist. There are young children, teenagers, and retirees, sports enthusiasts, and musicians.

During a blinding blizzard the doctor, wearing an old sheepskin coat and a red stocking cap, rode his snowmobile up and down the snow-deep streets making sure everyone had medicine, food, and warm blankets.

When my old oak tree fell during a storm, a teacher came by with his chain saw, cut it up in short pieces, and stacked it. The kids in the neighborhood took care of the small stuff.

When an accident cut the electrical wires in a house in our community, their neighbor ran a line from her house to theirs for forty-eight hours.

When I got all messed up on my computer (I'm a real dud about computers), the photographer came and got me straightened out in no time.

Everyone respects our privacy; we aren't buddy-buddy. Yet if I needed help, I could call on any one of them and they would come in a Midwest minute.

Our common bond is the lake. It's the scents and sounds of wildlife. It's a great blue heron sitting motionless on the dock. It's a full moon making a silver iridescent path across rippling waters. It's two swans; royalty sailing by.

Perhaps it's a spectacular sunset, cerulean, violet, and palest pink—so lovely, so fleeting, it's to weep.

Or maybe it is just the warm sunshine on the sand where you can sit and let the quiet wash over you.

It can be a winter storm when angry waves dash against rocks, and the fury of Lake Erie is frightening and exciting.

It can be a no man's-land when the lake freezes over, and you wonder if this is the way it looks on the surface of the moon.

It's the lake, always the same, always different, never ending. One after another we all gravitate to the lake.

My community—small town Midwest.

Decluttering

Magazines and television seem to be obsessed with the idea of decluttering. If I just follow a few simple rules, they suggest, I can declutter my home and make housework a Piece of Cake. It sounds like a plan.

Before getting up in the morning, if I am very careful, I can pull the covers up to my chin, slide out sideways, add pillows, and the bed is made. But just as I'm smoothing the sheet I see a squirrel balancing precariously on the slender branch of the maple tree. He shakes his bushy tail just enough to make it sway back and forth. I pull the quilt over my shoulders and scoot to the end of the bed. He is so funny he makes me laugh.

He sees his buddies scampering around the oak tree and decides to join them. They chase each other all the way to the top and back down. I think they are teenagers. I think they are playing cops and robbers. So much energy, so early in the morning!

I head for the shower. Here, to save both time and money, while I'm in the shower I can scrub the walls. And if I use the same cleaning product for both myself and the walls, it doubles my efficiency. Should I use my expensive jasmine body wash on the walls or Fantastic on myself? I opt for jasmine. In the shower, all the white tile, soft warm water, jasmine scented air, I'm in a state of euphoria. I hum the *Blue Danube*. Before I know it, I've used up all the hot water. The walls will have to wait.

The mirror is all fogged up. The best time to wipe it down. But to tell the truth I like it all murky. Looking into that cloudy mirror, I don't look half bad. I can almost believe that I was once not too bad looking.

After a muffin and a cup of coffee, I'm ready to continue decluttering. I have three boxes. One for Keepers, one for Throwaways, one for the Goodwill. Shoes, purses, hats (who wears hats?) go into the Goodwill. Here is a long red dress, not fire engine red, red, white, and blue red with gold threads through the filmy skirt. I place it in the Goodwill box. I wonder if I can still get into it? I pull off my sweatshirt and slip into it. It fits! I dance around the room. I hum Ravel's *Bolero*. I'm dancing with Bill. I think I'll keep it. Naw! I'm too old for the red dress. I take it off, fold it carefully, put it in the Goodwill box. I cover it with an old sweater.

"Let's go for an adventure walk."

I look up and there's my small grandson.

"I'm so busy! Look at all these clothes!"

"It's a glad day," he says. His blue eyes are pleading.

"OK." I take his hand and out we go.

He takes his red wagon because who knows what treasure you may find on a summer day. We head for the beach.

He finds driftwood that looks like an eagle, places it in the red wagon. He finds a dead bird, a small finch.

"I think I'll bury it in your garden."

"That's a good idea, beside the pink roses."

He places it carefully in the wagon.

He finds a blue feather. "A blue jay lost it," he says.

"Look what I found: red glass. That's hardest to find, isn't it Grandma? You carry the feather and the glass till we get to your house."

In the sand he sees a small blue truck. "Somebody lost it," he says. "Do you think he'll be back to look for it?"

"He probably will, just leave it."

"I'll put sticks around it so he'll find it better."

We head for home.

"I'll leave my treasures at your house. Dad says you have more room." He unloads his wagon in my garage.

"I'll take the blue feather and the red glass home to Mama. It will be a surprise!"

"That's a lovely idea."

He goes off, up the road pulling his wagon.

After cheese and crackers for lunch, I decide to sort the snapshots that have been accumulating for years. I haven't a clue where some of these pictures were taken. Trees, buildings, places, people long forgotten. Into the Throwaway.

Here are *very old pictures*. Small kids posed on velvet cushions, little button shoes, ruffles and ribbons, even on the boys. They all look scared. Men and women in strange looking black clothes. They all look like they're having digestive problems. They're hilarious! I suppose they are blood relatives. When I stop laughing, I put them in the Keepers box. You really shouldn't throw blood relatives away.

I open a photograph album. There I am on the beach with Bill. A small dark-haired boy with beautiful eyes calls from the water, "Look at me, Mama, look at me! Watch me, Daddy. I can put my head under water. I can swim Mama, watch me! Watch me!"

A little red-haired girl calls from the beach. "I helped him cause I'm bigger, Mama. I helped him learn to swim."

I flip the page. There I am again, same beach, same place, alone.

A little blond blue-eyed boy calls from the water. "Look at me, Grandma, look at me. I can swim. Watch me, watch me!"

Oh, I can't sort these. I'll get all weepy. I shove the pictures back in the box, push it under the table.

On the way past the window I think I see the eagle. I grab the binoculars and dash outside. There he is on top of the oak tree. He's awesome! So beautiful! So fierce! I stay outside until he flies away.

It's time for supper. I get my book, prop it on the table, heat a bowl of chicken soup, grab a few crackers. My book lasts longer than my soup. I sit idly thinking about my day. I have definitely flunked Decluttering and Piece of Cake. I wonder if when I draw my last breath I will regret that I never coordinated my clothes or, God forbid, that I never put my condiments in alphabetical order.

I put my soup bowl in the sink and go to the lake. There are two dark green metal chairs. The same two chairs my mother and father had when they sat in their back yard on summer evenings, a yard where lilacs grew and children were always welcome.

I pull up a chair, put my feet on the sea wall. The moon has turned the lake to silver. The hush of night fills me and surrounds me.

In a whispery voice I say:
"I see skies of blue, clouds of white.
Bright blessed day, dark sacred night.
And I say to myself,
What a wonderful world!
And I say to myself,
What a wonderful world!

Acknowledgments:

Some of these pieces were originally published in various magazines, newspapers, and journals. Publication details are noted when available.

Two Poems was first published in *The Eagle's Flight*, Volume 11, No. 3, September 1999.

Weird! was first published in *Lilith* magazine.

The Potter was first published in *Heartlands* magazine.

The Dahlias was first published in *Bend of the River* magazine.

Like Living in the Past was published in the newspaper.

Fragments was first published in *Heartlands Magazine*.

School Clothes Needed Altering In September was first published by *Bend of the River* magazine, Volume 27, No. 8, September, 1999

Fifty Year Member was first published by the First Presbyterian Church of Huron, Ohio in their monthly newsletter, December.

Fireworks, Never Forgotten Fourth was first published in the newspaper.

New Car was first published in *Home & Away* magazine

Palmolive Soap was entered into a company sponsored competition in 1930, and was awarded a $1,000 prize.

My Church (poem) was first published by the First Presbyterian Church of Huron in their monthly newsletter, December 2005.

The Sunday Feeling was first published by *Home Life* magazine, January 1957.

About the author:
(1912-2013)

Wilma (Hartley) Daugherty was born in East Palestine, Ohio. She was one of seven children growing up in a household surrounded by books and music. After graduating from high school in Alliance, Ohio, she attended Grove City College in western Pennsylvania. There, she met her husband Bill. Together, they built their first house on the lake, raised a family, and pursued their love of the arts.

After completing her Bachelor of Arts degree at Bowling Green State University, she taught third and fourth graders in Huron, Ohio for twenty-four years. Like Bill, her husband of fifty years, Wilma painted with oils and watercolors. She was also an avid writer of short stories and poems which have been collected into four books. Additionally, she wrote a children's book for the Merry-Go-Round Museum in Sandusky, Ohio.

Most of her adult life was spent in a house that overlooked Lake Erie. From her front porch she observed nature and delighted in the many moods of the constantly moving waters.

CPSIA information can be obtained
at www.ICGtesting.com
Printed in the USA
FFOW04n0836200816
26848FF